Thanks to the human heart by which we live,
Thanks to its tenderness, its joys, and fears,
To me the meanest flower that blows can give
Thoughts that do often lie too deep for tears.

William Wordsworth

For Dominic and Josh again

Making a cottage garden

FAITH AND GEOFF WHITEN

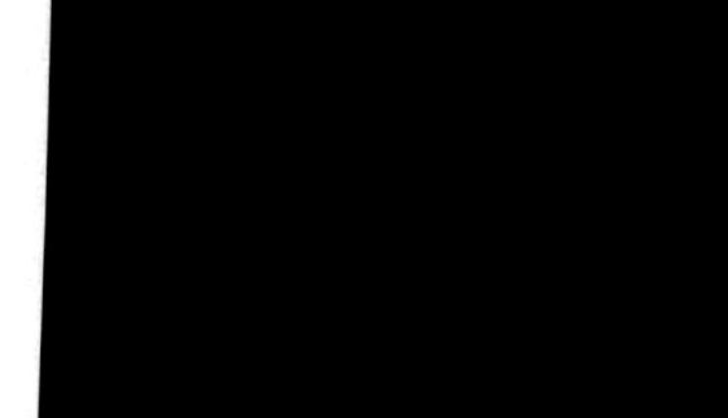

BELL & HYMAN

First published by Bell & Hyman 1985
Bell & Hyman Limited
Denmark House
37–39 Queen Elizabeth Street
London SE1 2QB

Reprinted 1986

Whiten, Faith
Making a cottage garden.
1. Gardening — Great Britain
2. Gardens — Great Britain — Design
I. Title II. Whiten, Geoff
712'.6'0941 SB453.3.G7

ISBN 0-7135-2513-4

ISBN 0 7135 2513 4

Designed by Malcolm Harvey Young

Original line artwork by Hilary Evans

Phototypeset by Tradespools Ltd, Frome, Somerset
Colour Reproduction by Positive Colour Ltd., Maldon, Essex
Produced in Portugal by Printer Portuguesa-Sintra

Contents

Foreword

IN THIS COUNTRY we treasure and relish our traditions. National and local, they are reflected in almost every facet of our lives. One of our great national pastimes, gardening, has as its main tradition the cottage garden: a jumble of colours most of the year, a profusion of old favourite plants, a source of sweet scent.

Evocative of all this is the opening chapter of Faith and Geoff Whiten's book on the cottage garden. The authors convey the essence of a cottage garden, bringing it verbally to life, and they show, in the following chapters, how to bring it actually to life, without undue difficulty and not necessarily in the country, but just as appropriately in a city or a suburb.

The book exudes their love of cottage gardens and their deep knowledge of the best available varieties of plants suitable, by tradition, for such a garden; varieties, which, as they put it, maintain the spirit of the old plants.

The pleasure that can be derived from a deliberately random planting of the wide range of appropriate plants is lovingly conveyed, and encouragement is given to experiment with planting schemes, to do your own thing.

This book is a worthy contribution to our garden literature, and no one could be better qualified to write it than the authors, who have won two gold medals at Chelsea, the second for just such a garden, splendidly conceived and planted, and who wrote *The Chelsea Flower Show*, a fascinating book telling not only the history, but the inner workings of the show.

Their latest book is equally fascinating, equally well written, and equally enjoyable whether you want to make a cottage garden or just to dream what fun that would be.

Aberconway

The Lord Aberconway,
President Emeritus,
The Royal Horticultural Society

Introduction

HAVING EXHIBITED gardens at the Chelsea Show for a number of years, we could not resist rising to a challenge to attempt our most ambitious undertaking yet — to recreate a cottage garden to demonstrate that this traditional style, with its old-fashioned flowers, is still appropriate today and can be achieved by almost anyone in almost any setting.

To our gratitude, the Halifax Building Society had the great courage to embark on the project with us, and we therefore set about adapting the traditions of the nineteenth century and even earlier to create a design that would offer the sort of features that we demand of a garden now, whilst losing none of the old-world charm and appeal.

We also sought materials that would have the right look, yet would be available to home gardeners up and down the country and — most important of all — we started to ascertain which were the authentic

cottage garden plants and to identify those that can still be obtained today. To our surprise, a great many survive. They can be bought as plants from garden centres and specialist mail order nurseries and as bulbs and seeds from supermarkets as well as horticultural shops.

The distinctive character of cottage planting relies on a happy, informal mixture of shrubs, climbers, perennials, biennials, annuals, bulbs, herbs (both culinary and medicinal) and even fruit to achieve its effect. This made it quite an undertaking not only to research and identify plants, but then to locate them and have them grown on for showing at Chelsea in late May. The task proved an enjoyable one, but it would have been impossible without help — not only the invaluable support of the Halifax but also advice from some distinguished horticulturists and practical assistance from many specialists in supplying and growing on plants.

At the Show, we found that the cottage style appealed to keen gardeners and to the less knowledgeable, for everyone knew well at least some of the 'flowers that Granny grew' and many asked for more information about the cottage plants — where to get them, how to grow them — and, in short, how to make a cottage garden. We hope this is the kind of thing they had in mind . . .

Faith and Geoff Whiten

THE ADVANTAGES of home ownership are many and varied, but for a lot of people the appeal lies simply in the prospect of living in their own house with its own garden. The Halifax Building Society has always recognized the value that owners of properties of all types and sizes place on their garden, and the pleasure they get from making their surroundings more beautiful. An attractive garden is capable not only of improving the quality of everyday life, but also of enhancing the general appearance of the property which itself represents the major investment that most people are ever likely to undertake.

The cottage garden is a uniquely English phenomenon that, although steeped in tradition, is nevertheless still relevant today — and especially for the ordinary householder, for cottage gardens were created not by the wealthy owners of great estates but by artisans, smallholders and craftsmen and their families — in town as well as in the country.

The Halifax Cottage Garden at the prestigious Chelsea Flower Show was welcomed by thousands of such householders, who recognized that this style of garden, with all its old-fashioned charm, could be adapted to almost any small plot in any location. We hope that they will welcome equally the more detailed information and advice offered by this book.

The enthusiasm for our Cottage Garden has encouraged us to further endeavours at the Chelsea Show, for the Society continues in its efforts to make a significant contribution to our environment and quality of life by demonstrating to existing and future homeowners how they can make the most of their garden.

The Halifax Building Society

Acknowledgements

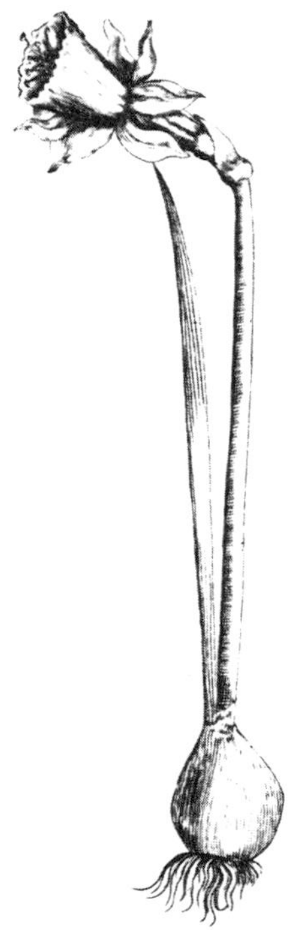

WE WOULD very much like to thank the following for all their help, advice and encouragement both in the preparation of this book and the creation of the cottage garden at Chelsea, which started it all . . . Lord Aberconway, who presented us with the challenge; Chris Brickell, Director-General of the RHS and Ray Waite of Wisley Garden; Anne Scott-James for her personal advice and her book 'The Cottage Garden'; the Halifax Building Society, Dick Spelman, Sue Bamford and their colleagues; Tony Hender and Ralph Gould of Hurst Seeds; Laurence Flatman and Adrian Bloom; John Mattock; John Cowell, Allan Sawyer and their colleagues at the RHS; Brent Elliott of the Lindley Library; Frederic Doerflinger of the Bulb Information Desk; David Wilkinson and Geoff Worrall of Bradstone; David Reed and Barry Holliman for their invaluable practical help; Redland Bricks and Stapeley Water Gardens for technical assistance; Graham Richardson and Patrick Johns for their photography and Geest Horticulture for their extremely generous help with illustrations.

Finally, a special thank you to Clive Stickland for research, Ann Stickland for typing and both of them for their enthusiasm, matched only by that of Connie Austen Smith, our editor.

he cottage garden tradition

FROM TIME TO TIME most of us indulge in a sentimental longing to recapture a way of life that seems almost to have disappeared. We dream about living in a little thatched cottage nestling among rolling fields and hills, leading a simple, peaceful existence uncluttered by the noise, bustle and stress that appear to be inescapable features of work, entertainment and even domestic life in the 1980s.

Appealing though the dream may be, we would probably ultimately admit to ourselves that it is only that — a charming, appealing dream. If forced to make a decision, we may well prove loth to give up such creature comforts as running water, central heating and the convenience of shops, schools and public transport just around the corner.

And yet there is a way in which at least part of that vision, however unashamedly romantic, can be made to come true, for the traditional cottage garden with its profusion of sweet smelling, old-fashioned flowers does not involve great investment, nor great physical sacrifice. The cottage garden is not an impossible dream, but an achievable aim — and not only for those who really do live in a small house in the country. There is no reason why the cottage style of garden should not flourish in modern plots on new housing estates, in a back yard in the city or beside a bungalow in the suburbs.

That the mood and character of a cottage garden could exist in a setting other than the gentle English rural scene and at a time later than the early 1900s is by no means a unique or revolutionary idea; sometimes its spirit is captured — perhaps unconsciously or instinctively — in the most unexpected places.

For instance our own fondness for cottage gardens developed from very different backgrounds — one, predictably perhaps, from a country childhood amidst cornfields and hedgerows and beside the village pond, but the other from the more unexpected setting of the garden of a rambling Victorian house in the suburbs of south east London.

Even in this suburban setting simple, old-fashioned flowers became an intrinsic part of everyday life. In summer there were London pride, lords and ladies and 'soldiers and sailors'; the abundance of roses were made to yield their petals to be mixed with water in jars and rusty tins and left to

The idyllic image of a cottage in the country — a painting by Arthur Stanley Wilkinson

brew into 'rose scent'. Then there was lilac and the huge mock orange blossom bush; the rich, curled, velvety purple petals of 'flags' and, perhaps best of all, the fat, globular, red-tinged buds of peonies, the frilly edges unfolding with their promise of those lovely full blooms the colour of Crimson Lake in the paint box.

In colder months there were chrysanthemums and wallflowers, and in spring the daffodils grown from bulbs brought home from school competitions; all year round there were the familiar bent and gnarled branches of the Victoria plum tree. There was rarely a crop of plums for the picking, but who cared because the gum that seeped from the trunk could be picked and rolled into squashy balls.

Crown imperial

All this may have been suburbia in the 1950s, but there was something of the spirit of the cottage garden there — the pleasure of living with traditional, well-loved flowers that became indicators of the seasons and were woven into the fabric of everyday life. Such a garden, such plants sink into the memory. It is hardly surprising that when, as adults, we have a garden of our own, we want to grow those fondly familiar plants and maybe even pass the tradition on to our children.

It is not difficult to understand how cottage gardens must have developed. As a matter of tradition and instinct people would grow the same flowers for generation after generation. Of course, new introductions would appear — plants that originated in the hedgerows or meadows, that were brought back to settle in Britain from plant hunting expeditions around the world, and even probably the occasional cutting or root culled from the garden of the 'big house'. All would have to take their chance alongside the existing inhabitants, and if they have survived as part of the tradition of cottage gardens it is because they have proved themselves to be appealing to look at and capable of flourishing without undue fuss and attention.

Cottage plants were a legacy not only of beauty and emotional attachment, but of real usefulness. Obviously, fruit and vegetables were grown to be eaten, but many plants that we regard as entirely ornamental were prized for their uses in cooking, preserving and medicine. The theory was that if a plant had a beautiful, brightly coloured flower, nature intended people's attention to be drawn to it, to seek its powers and uses.

There was much wisdom and sound commonsense in the traditional applications of plants, but they were also the subject of a number of old wives' tales. Some of them — mostly associated with the ability of flowers to help or hinder romance — were harmless and rather charming as, too, are the stories about the origins of the plants and their names and the everyday experiences and emotions that they came to symbolize.

Maybe it is mere romantic nostalgia that attracts us to the folklore as well as to the garden value of the plants, but there is nothing wrong in that — and even less wrong with wishing to feel a sense of participation in a national rural tradition which can still be recreated and cherished in an age of fast cars, home computers and washing-up machines.

When we visualize the cottage garden of our dreams, we probably imagine a soft, pretty patchwork of roses round the door, sweet honeysuckle, pinks and hollyhocks — but this may be a rather vague and hazy image, so where and how do you actually start to make a cottage garden? What exactly did cottage gardens look like? What were the traditional flowers, and how can that look be achieved with the plants and materials readily available today in cities, towns and suburbs as well as the countryside?

When we embarked on the creation of a cottage garden that could be achieved and enjoyed by the ordinary modern homeowner these were questions that demanded answers, and we started to search for them by looking at illustrations of some authentic originals and trying to understand the way in which cottage gardens developed over hundreds of years.

From references in Chaucer's *Canterbury Tales*, we learn that, even in medieval times, some sort of yard existed around the cottage of the small farmer or husbandman. Whilst much of the space was given over to livestock, there was also evidently a vegetable plot and a patch of herbs for culinary and medicinal purposes. Chaucer mentions centaury, fumitory, elderberries, spurge laurel, caper spurge, blackthorn berries and ground-ivy amongst others.

Probably the earliest evidence that can be of help in our quest for a model for the modern cottage garden is found in the Elizabethan era of Merrie England and William Shakespeare. In fact, we can link the subject with Shakespeare's work — where there are many references to the cottage flowers — and also with his life, for one of the best surviving examples of an Elizabethan cottage garden is the family home of Anne Hathaway at Shottery near Stratford-on-Avon. The garden has been maintained in much the same way for hundreds of years, and there is still a profusion of familiar flowers and herbs such as wallflowers, phlox, delphiniums, lupins and hollyhocks, sheltering behind neatly clipped hedges.

We can discover a great deal more about the plants grown in the late sixteenth and early seventeenth century thanks to two remarkable writers whose work is just as lively and informative today as when it was originally produced.

John Gerard was a herbalist who, in 1597, published *The Herball or General Historie of Plantes*. His writing is suffused with his love of plants and his wry, humorous observations of humanity and the wealth of small detail he includes make the book a joy to read for anyone interested in traditional plants and their uses.

The style and quality of his writing is worth appreciating too, as this extract from his introduction to the Herbal illustrates:

> What greater delight is there than to behold the earth apparelled with plants, as with a robe of embroidered worke, set out with Orient pearles and garnished with great diversitie of rare and costly jewels?

Perhaps less entertaining, but equally informative, is John Parkinson's *Paradisi in Sole, Paradisus Terrestris*, published in 1629. Interestingly, Parkinson describes as traditional many English flowers for which we might use exactly the same expression today — plants like primroses, cowslips, rose campion, wallflowers, violets, columbine, poppies, carnations and pinks (which were known as gillyflowers). However, although these old-fashioned cottage flowers are mentioned, the book was really designed for the wealthy and often aristocratic owners of large houses and estates, amongst whom it was fashionable to create a pleasure garden or park, and cottage gardens have never been the province of such people.

Martagon lily bulb

Indeed, as Anne Scott-James points out in her authoritative book, *The Cottage Garden* (Allen Lane, 1981), it is precisely because cottage gardens were created by artisans, village craftsmen, small farmers and husbandmen

Anne Hathaway's cottage at Shottery near Stratford-on-Avon

(although hardly by the very poorest and most ignorant farm labourers) that we have only fragmentary evidence of their history and appearance over a long period of time.

Nevertheless, we do know that the garden was always an important source of food, and that as well as basic vegetables, cottagers grew a wide range of herbs that were employed in many ways — in cooking; for strewing on the floor to disinfect and discourage fleas and make the cottage smell sweet; for stuffing mattresses; as a stimulant in wine and for medicinal purposes, often being mixed with boiling water to make an infusion or herb tea.

Growing vegetables was traditionally the responsibility of the man of the house, and it was usually his wife who would plant flowers purely for their beauty and ornamental value. The effect was always informal, for such design concepts as parterres, knot gardens and symmetrical beds were very much the province of the gentry and the wealthy. Rather than stiff, formal plants the country cottage plot boasted the simple flowers of the countryside — primroses, violets, jonquils, pinks, larkspur, lavender, foxgloves, crown imperials and lovely old-fashioned roses. Even these were pressed into uses hardly heard of today: at one time violets were used in salads, stuffings and sauces, made into syrup and strewn on the floor.

In searching for inspiration for a modern cottage garden we can look not only to these rural traditions but also the town-dwelling cottage gardeners.

In the eighteenth century the hobby of 'floristry' really took a hold, having been introduced to Britain by Flemish and French artisans — especially weavers — who came to work here. The term florist had nothing to do with flower arranging or flower shops, as we might understand it, but rather with the occupation of breeding selected flowers to develop ever more colourful, shapely or flamboyant blooms, and in showing those prize blooms in competitions — the forerunners of the flower shows that are now held every summer in almost every town, village and suburb.

Floristry was particularly prevalent in the north of England, and in areas where the weavers worked. They were not alone in practising the art of floristry, but because they worked at home in small terraced houses with a back yard (the sort of house that estate agents nowadays describe as an 'artisan's cottage') they were always on hand to tend and cosset their prize blooms and react quickly to any change in the weather. Much to the frustration of their competitors, it was, consequently, the weavers who almost inevitably carried off all the prizes.

Initially the selection of florist's flowers was quite wide, but it was eventually reduced to just eight — anemone, auricula, carnation, hyacinth, pink, polyanthus, ranunculus and tulip. The tradition flourished right through to the mid nineteenth century and even later, but the expansion of industry eventually overtook the florists' gentle art. The weavers were gradually absorbed into the factories and so, sadly, the hobby faded away, together with many of the flower varieties they had bred.

This watercolour by Arthur Claude Strachan illustrates both the luxuriance and informality of the traditional cottage garden style

To a large extent our idea of the idyllic cottage garden has its roots in a relatively recent period — the second half of the nineteenth century. Perhaps in reaction to the industrial revolution, the simple life of the countryside was widely adopted as an idealistic theme by artists, poets and writers. Some were sentimental in their approach, drawn to the romantic image of a rural family who, although poor, were content with their lot and with their peaceful existence in the healthy fresh air amidst beautiful scenery. However, others were more objective and it is their work, demonstrating real sympathy for people and an appreciation of the simple, genuine beauty of cottage gardens, that lives on; that, indeed, becomes more and more popular as modern life becomes more sophisticated and fast-moving.

Among the painters, there was interesting work by Myles Birket Foster and Stanley Wilkinson and others, but probably best loved and most informative are the water colours of Helen Allingham, which, for all their prettiness, are sympathetic rather than sentimental. Her paintings show old ladies gossiping at the garden gate; washing blowing on the line; little girls dressed in bonnet, smock and boots. The flowers are unmistakably drawn from real-life observation. Pansies, pinks, iris, tumbling roses, foxgloves, cornflowers, delphiniums all merge in a soft tapestry of colour; sunflowers nod over the hawthorn hedge and apples ripen on the tree.

Writers who took up the countryside theme also tended to divide into the romantic and the more realistic. Firmly in the latter category are two who are especially interesting because they knew cottage life at first hand.

Flora Thompson's trilogy *Lark Rise to Candleford* contains a wealth of unsentimental detail not only about the cottages and their gardens, but also about the cottagers who lived in and tended them. For them, life was often harsh — a constant struggle to overcome poverty and need whilst at the same time maintaining human dignity. A family might keep a few chickens, and would certainly keep a pig fattening in a lean-to sty at the back of the house. This creature was their pride and joy whilst alive and their staple diet when dead; when they could simply not afford to buy nourishing food the baker or miller would give credit in return for the promise of a portion of the pig when it was killed.

Fritillaries

The manure and 'oozings' from the sty were heaped up with household refuse to make compost for the garden, and this, together with rich, dark 'night soil' from the privy (often moved around to benefit the whole plot) provided fertilizer for growing herbs and vegetables (especially cabbage) and also flowers, grown and tended, still, by the woman of the house.

John Clare was a Victorian poet who wrote simply and unpretentiously about his own experience and observations growing up and living in the villages of Northamptonshire. Some literary scholars have considered that a person of his rural background must have lacked sufficient intellectual and emotional refinement to experience a strong, deep link between nature and human emotions — the theme of the work of the Romantic poets like Wordsworth. However, there is touching freshness in his work even if he did dispense with the refinements of grammar and punctuation.

> I always feel delighted when an object in nature brings up in ones mind an image of poetry that describes it from some favourite Author . . . . The clown knows nothing of these pleasures . . . . he knows they are flowers and just turns an eye on them and plods bye. Therefore as I said before to look on nature with a poetic eye magnifys the pleasure she herself being the very essence and soul of poesy.

Eventually, the interest in cottage gardens and their exuberant, informal style of planting spread from the writers and painters to a small, select succession of horticulturists.

In 1883, William Robinson published *The English Flower Garden*, and the influence of his ideas and commendation of the cottage style is still felt today:

> English cottage gardens are never bare and seldom ugly. Those who look at sea or sky or wood see beauty that no art can show; but among the things made by man nothing is prettier than an English cottage garden, and they often teach lessons that 'great' gardeners should learn, and are pretty from snowdrop time till the Fuchsia bushes bloom nearly into winter. We do not see the same thing in other lands . . .

Like William Robinson, Gertrude Jekyll — who designed many gardens for houses created by the great architect Lutyens — took the simple beauty of the soft cottage style and developed it on a grander scale, her planting schemes demonstrating particular feeling for delicacy of colour and texture and experimentation with colour themes.

This gentrification of the cottage garden continued to stunning effect in the garden created by Vita Sackville-West at Sissinghurst. She loved the tumbling, rambling, old-fashioned flowers and was always experimenting with some new theme of shape, perfume or colour in the small 'enclosures' into which the garden was divided.

Although the work of all three was on quite a grand scale and embodied a rather 'gentrified' approach, their gardens and their message were in stark contrast to the way in which the mainstream of gardening was developing at the time. Robinson, for instance, was critical of the stiff, extreme formality of Victorian carpet bedding, and of the fact that gardens had become status symbols, with snob value attached to expensive and sophisticated stove houses where tender, exotic subjects like orchids would be grown. In contrast, he maintained that part of the charm of cottage gardens was that they 'let the flowers tell their story to the heart.'

Rigid, labour-intensive formality still predominates in many parks and gardens today — the very opposite of the soft, luxuriant planting of the cottage garden, where there is no shrub border, nor herbaceous border; no summer bedding in stiff rows and patterns. Instead, only the effect so perfectly observed by Flora Thompson in *Candleford Green*:

> Narrow paths between high, built-up banks supporting flower borders, crowded with jonquils, auriculas, forget-me-nots and other spring flowers, led from one part of the garden to another. One winding path led to the earth closet in its bower of nut trees half-way down the garden, another to the vegetable garden and on to the rough grass plot before the beehives. Between

'Madonna Lilies' by E. A. Chadwick

each section were thick groves of bushes with ferns and capers and Solomon's seal, so closed in that the long, rough grass there was always damp. Wasted ground, a good gardener might have said, but delightful in its cool, green shadiness.

Nearer the house was a portion given up entirely to flowers, not growing in beds or borders, but crammed together in an irregular square, where they bloomed in half-wild profusion. There were rose bushes there and lavender and rosemary and a bush apple-tree which bore the little red and yellow streaked apples in later summer, and Michaelmas daisies and red-hot pokers and old-fashioned pompom dahlias in autumn and peonies and pinks already budding.

An old man in the village came one day a week to till the vegetable garden, but the flower garden was no one's special business . . . . the flowers grew just as they would in crowded masses, perfect in their imperfection.

The 'white' garden at Sissinghurst created by Vita Sackville-West

Design and practical planning

HAVING FORMED A PICTURE of how cottage gardens looked some one hundred years ago, it is necessary to face perhaps the most daunting task in the process of making a cottage garden; that of translating the mood and spirit, the essential 'look' of a tradition that reached its heyday in a very different society from our own, into a garden that is practical to achieve and maintain here and now.

Gardens that were made in the nineteenth century were right for their time and the way of life of their owners, and it is hardly practical to attempt to recreate an *exactly* faithful reproduction of one of those romantic water colour paintings.

Besides, even if such a recreation were possible in practical terms, it would be rather like painting by numbers instead of by instinct and inspiration. Like the rooms of a house, a garden should surely — and probably does, whether or not we intend it to — reflect the personality of its creator or creators. So, perhaps our ultimate aim should be a garden that is unmistakably in the cottage style, that includes the authentic cottage plants that are still available and can be grown today, but that also has personal touches which give it a stamp of individuality.

In addition, there are sound practical reasons for adapting the cottage garden to suit our way of life. It should not be necessary to give up the facilities and advantages that we expect a garden to offer in order to create a timepiece that is visually romantic and nostalgic, but unusable for all those practical things like sitting and eating outside, hanging out the washing and storing the tools.

Nor do we necessarily have time for a labour-intensive garden. Limited time available for gardening and the desire to simply sit back and enjoy the plants should not prevent you from having a garden in the cottage style — far from it. Cottagers, too, were busy people with limited resources and many demands on their time — not least the demands of earning a living and feeding and clothing the family.

The actual ground plan of the traditional cottage garden was fairly basic. Although, of course, it would vary, it is necessary for our purpose to take a rather generalized outline — one that was very frequently adhered to — and use it as a starting point for a modern garden in the cottage style.

Before dealing in much greater detail with back gardens, it is worth taking a look at the very small area of ornamental garden that was often found at the front of the cottage, for this does lend itself much more readily to virtual reproduction in the small front gardens that so often come with a terraced house, or even with larger houses, both new and old.

Of course, there were very often roses round the door, and in the limited area for plants there might be a bold clump of hollyhocks or foxgloves with something shorter like pyrethrum daisies and sweet William. There might, too, be a bold shrub such as hydrangea and possibly clay flower pots containing geraniums. The material used for the path to the front door would vary from county to county. In a natural stone area like the Cotswolds it might be made from random slabs of the warm, honey coloured stone, whilst in Kent or Sussex bricks would be laid, and moss allowed to grow through the slightly irregular joints.

There was frequently a fence or low wall separating the garden from the lane, recalling the childhood pleasure of peeking over the garden wall to see what adventures lay beyond. Plants might grow in and on the wall, spilling over the top or self-seeding to scatter in colonies at the bottom, helping to create that cheerful, informal, essentially cottagey look.

Other cottages had much larger front gardens — indeed the greater part of their plot was situated to the front of the house, with a smaller yard at the back accommodating the pig in its sty, perhaps some beehives, and certainly an earth closet.

Whether the main, large area of garden was situated to the front or back of the house, it most often followed the general, very basic outline that we are taking as our starting point — quite simply a straight path up the middle with plants spilling over from wide beds on either side. This layout, however, offers little scope to do anything except grow plants, and the modern garden owner would probably consider it too restrictive. Moreover, the prospect of vast areas of plant beds can be daunting, too, as they need filling and subsequent tending — particularly perhaps for new gardeners who love the old-fashioned flowers but do not have a great deal of experience of growing them, or of keeping a garden going all year round.

Another major change of emphasis in this book is from the productive to the ornamental. Traditionally, flowers of all kinds, fruit and vegetables were all considered equally important, but there are many other sources of reference on how to grow vegetables, and here we are concerned mostly with how the authentic ornamental cottage plants can be used today, when it is no longer essential to 'grow your own'.

So, how do we solve this problem? How to take the traditional and, without losing its feel or character, create a design that provides the right setting for the traditional plants, yet can meet the practical needs of modern householders, whether their property is in town or country, new or old.

Firstly it is wise to consider that gardens these days are not necessarily surrounded by others of similar style, as those of the cottages in a village

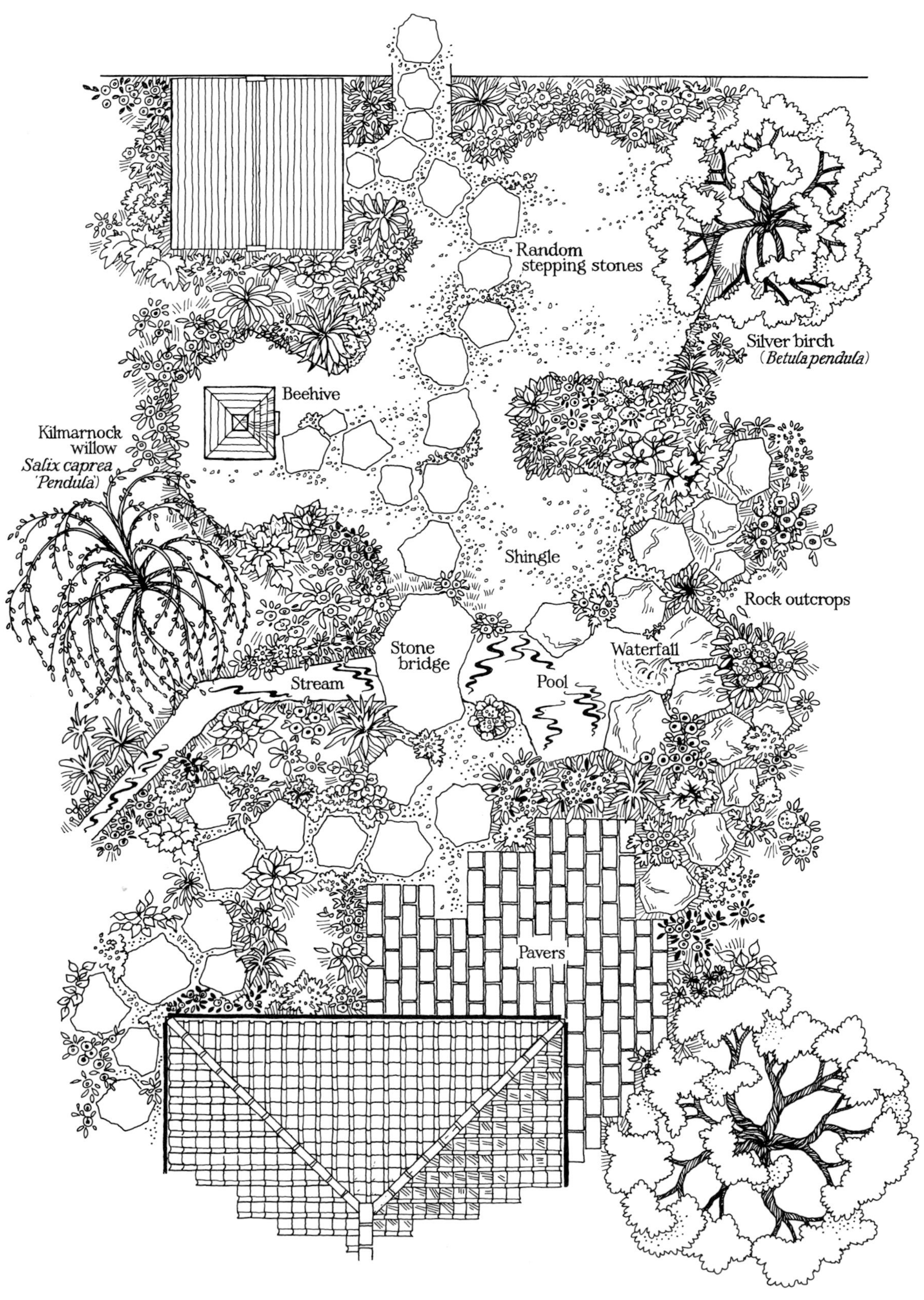
Random
stepping stones
Silver birch
(Betula pendula)
Beehive
Kilmarnock
willow
Salix caprea
'Pendula'
Shingle
Rock outcrops
Stone
bridge
Waterfall
Stream
Pool
Pavers

would have been. There, plants merged in friendly familiarity at the boundaries, being 'borrowed' by neighbours as part of the background to their own plot.

The garden next to your own might be quite uncultivated, or a formal conglomeration of brightly coloured bedding plants standing to attention. It may be that only a chain link fence separates your plot from a patchwork of lawns so familiar on new housing developments — that sea of green

The cottage garden at Chelsea, where planting spreads outward and upward from the central path

A design based on the Chelsea garden, where the emphasis was on ornamental features including a stream with a stone bridge, a rock feature with waterfall, a garden building in traditional style and plant areas that curve informally, spilling over into shingled surfaces

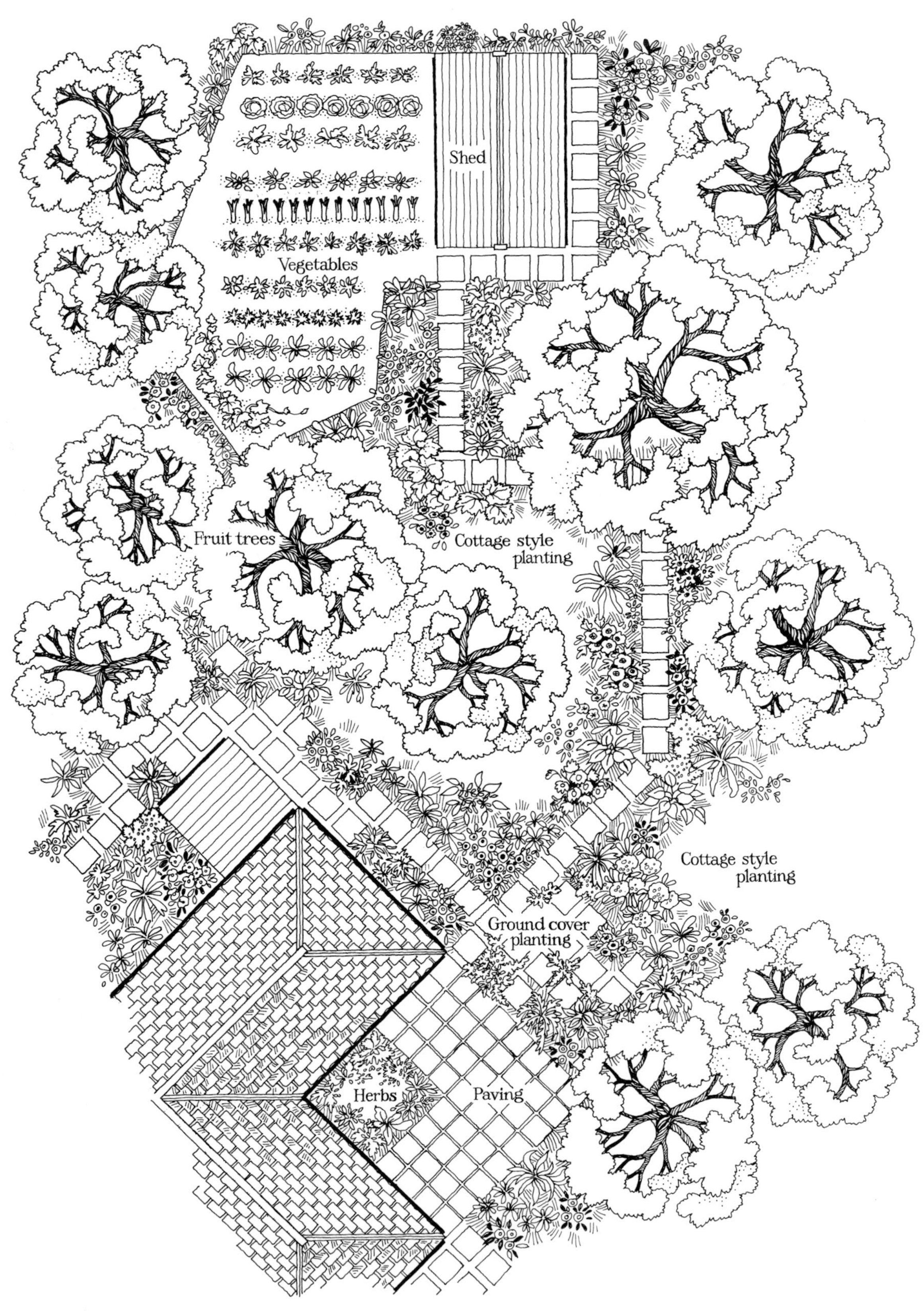
Shed
Vegetables
Fruit trees
Cottage style planting
Cottage style planting
Ground cover planting
Herbs
Paving

punctuated only by rotary clothes dryers or hedges of wispy Leyland cypresses.

All this means that if the setting is far from rural, you may need to work harder to make your layout intimate and self-contained, so that it actually works in capturing the atmosphere of a country cottage garden when you are in it.

When seeking our own solution to these problems we took as the starting point the basic cottage layout which has a path straight up the centre of the plot. We decided to expand outward from that central line, not losing its sense altogether but extending it to create more space for moving around the garden, giving access to plant areas that are manageable in size and providing somewhere to sit, storage for tools and features such as an ornamental pond and stream.

Standing at the front of the garden and looking through to the back, the clear, central line of vision is still fairly flat, the shape building upwards and outwards towards the side boundaries, creating a soft framework that could become quite a dense visual screen at the outer edges. This creates a feeling of intimacy, allows the plants to be positioned and to compose themselves so that each can be seen and appreciated and gives the opportunity of using many low-growing plants that will spill over paths and edges, softening the overall appearance of the garden and helping to determine its cottagey character.

This approach places a definite emphasis on the ornamental, although there is a beehive and fruit is grown together with the flowers. For a garden that is more productive, a number of fruit trees could be planted and a vegetable plot cultivated at the far end of the garden, in an open position. Although Victorian cottagers were unlikely to have possessed a greenhouse, nowadays one might be considered an important facility for growing crops such as cucumbers and tomatoes and raising half-hardy annuals from seed, and this would logically be located beside the vegetable plot — again in an open, sunny location.

A very large vegetable plot could be divided by paths to create beds of manageable size; brick paths would be most authentic, but a man-made paving slab that gives the impression of brick or natural stone is a good alternative. However, the plot should not be designed in too formal a manner — the French parterre style is highly decorative, but rather too genteel and raised beds, also, are rather too elaborate.

Few cottage gardens seem to have featured a lawn; more likely to be found were areas of rough grass under trees or in places where nothing much else grew. Nevertheless, there are paintings of children sitting on a lawn in a cottagey garden, its edges bordered by plant beds spilling over with a profusion of old-fashioned flowers. Such a scene probably encompasses the two important points about lawns — firstly, if you have young children, an open area of grass does offer somewhere for them to play and secondly, a lawn as a feature of a cottage garden should be informal in shape, yet uncluttered with fussy little beds; rather it should be bordered by quite dense planting in the traditional way.

This design for a larger, mature garden places the emphasis on production. Not only are there established fruit trees and a vegetable plot with shed or greenhouse, but space is also devoted to flowering plants and herbs, and there is room to sit outside

Random York stepping stones are combined with Set pavers which, although man-made, have the appearance of natural stone

Paving set in shingle and softened by scattered planting

Wattle fencing blends well in this corner of an informal garden; although very traditional, nowadays wattle can be hard to obtain

A garden store built from Traditional Walling incorporates an old privy door, recreating the cottage atmosphere

The design of a cottage garden should, like any other style of plot, follow basic principles regarding the choice of features and materials to be included and the way in which all the components of the garden are brought together. All the features should be in scale, and that scale a human one, so that people feel comfortable; the design should not look too fussy or over-complicated and the materials and plants should blend and complement each other.

However, the creation of a cottage garden introduces an extra dimension, for not only should all the features blend, but they should be appropriate for this distinctive style of garden. If we were creating an exact replica of an authentic nineteenth century cottage garden, the materials to be used would be dictated by our model, and although the 'shopping list' might be easy to write, the actual goods might prove very difficult to obtain. Instead, we must take a more realistic approach and, looking around at all the materials that are actually available from garden centres and even builders' merchants, must select those that are most appropriate to our purpose — that offer the nearest modern equivalent of the cottage style, and can happily be worked into a scheme. Remember, too, that cottagers used whatever materials were available to them, and sometimes used them in a fairly haphazard way, so it is best to avoid making features in the garden look too carefully composed.

Anemones

The first part of the planning is in the framework — the structural features including walling, paving and fencing. Natural stone is not so widely available these days, and can be very expensive; moreover, traditional drystone walling must be built properly, which demands special skills and techniques. However, man-made alternatives can look convincingly like natural stone, especially if they are cast from natural stone masters, and they are easier to obtain and handle.

Old bricks are another good alternative. If you find an old house that is being demolished, and can obtain some old stock bricks, then they are ideal to clean up and re-use, making new brickwork look instantly old and weathered. If you have to buy new, choose bricks with subtle colouring, and if you are laying bricks as paving, then ascertain from the builder's merchant that they are sufficiently hard to withstand frost and pedestrian traffic.

Paving for a cottage garden is a rather different technique from the usual patio, which demands neatly pointed joints. Instead, you could lay an informal but balanced mixture of, say, a few slabs of old York paving with bricks, or again you could go for a man-made slab cast from natural stone, with the textured profile and weathered colouring of the real thing. In either case, lay the paving to a mortar bed, as described in the next chapter, but you can then break the rules by sprinkling soil between the joints, as a habitat for moss or other plants.

In any case, it is essential to leave out the occasional slab or group of slabs in a convenient position to create a plant pocket for low-growing aromatic plants like thyme or those that thrive in dry soil like stonecrop, sempervivum or *Campanula carpatica*.

Gravel or shingle makes an excellent companion ground covering for paving, creating a change in surface texture and a softer look. A fine, flattish pebble is better than pea shingle as it is more inclined to stay put. You can choose a colour that blends with your paving (cream or pinkish red are attractive) and phase it in around stepping stones, creating wider areas between path and plant beds.

It is wise to clear the ground of perennial weeds before spreading shingle, and then to spread a maximum depth of 2 inches (5 cm). Once it is in position, sprinkle seeds of an annual like alyssum or Virginia stock and they will grow through the shingle. Such areas should not be regarded as suitable for heavy pedestrian traffic, but they can certainly be walked on and provide a base for a garden seat, if required. Where shingled area and plant beds meet, the planting can be phased in to create an irregular edge softened by traditional, low-growing cottage plants.

Fencing can be something of a problem. It is still possible to obtain traditional rural fencing like woven rush or wattle hurdles, but they are not widely available and are not terribly durable. Moreover, on a new housing development or in a suburban street, they might look just a little too incongruous. A simple trellis structure clothed in climbers is perhaps ideal, but if you want a solid screen, then of all the types of fencing available from garden centres, the vertical 'close board' type, in individual boards or as fence panels, is probably the most neutral and would blend most easily.

Sometimes fencing panels come in a rather strong golden shade, and you may want to stain them a darker colour to help them blend into the background. If you do so, be very careful about planting immediately afterwards, for some preservatives (especially creosote) are harmful to plants, and should be allowed to weather before coming into contact with them.

Probably better still than a fence — even one clothed in climbers — is a hedge. In a cottage garden, Leyland cypresses are definitely out, and besides, there are so many more attractive alternatives. The most traditional hedge for cottages was hawthorn, also known as quickthorn. Plants should be positioned 1 foot (30 cm) apart, and the hedge will reach between 5 and 8 feet (1.5–2.5 m) tall. Other cottagey plants suitable for hedging include sea buckthorn, roses, lavender, rosemary, yew, beech, holly and hardy fuchsias.

Of the features within the garden, a shed or garden building might ideally be constructed using old bricks or stone and old roof tiles, so that it looks a little like an old privy. For our own cottage garden, we were lucky enough to find an old privy door, which lent an air of authenticity! Failing this, you most certainly should avoid Swiss chalets, log cabins, and reproductions of genteel period pieces that would have looked more at home gracing the grounds of a stately home than a humble cottager's back yard. Better to settle for a plain shed in ordinary softwood and plant climbers to clothe it; there are several recommendations in the chapter devoted to climbing plants, but a good choice might be ivy or *Clematis montana*.

Simple toadstool seats set in a garden which uses natural timber and indigenous plants to create a pleasing rural atmosphere

A rustic pergola in a corner of the same garden

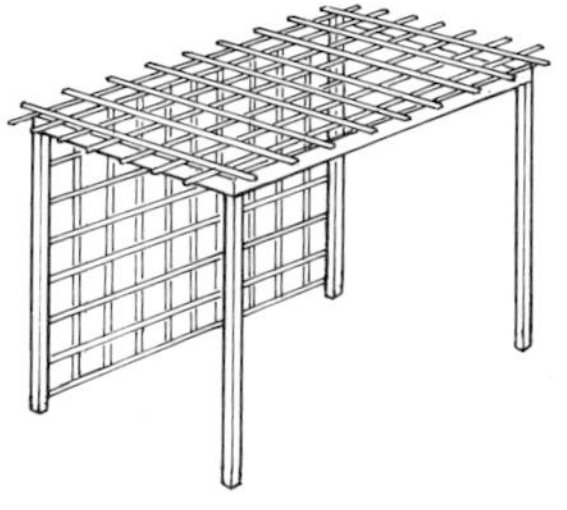

For a much lighter structure, a very simple rustic arch makes an attractive feature to span a pathway. Larch poles can be used for the basic construction, and can be clothed in rambling roses or honeysuckle. Even more appealing, and very romantic, is the traditional cottage arbour — a structure formed by climbers densely clothing a simple timber framework consisting of three sides and a roof, a seat being placed beneath. Again, the most traditional plants were honeysuckle and the sweetbriar rose, but clematis, jasmine and vines could also be planted. An arbour would make a charming focal point in the garden, and if your plot slopes, you could even create a 'dell' with rough cut grass, where the arbour becomes a 'secret' hideaway.

If you simply want garden furniture for sitting outside — either lounging or dining — then, again, it should be in keeping, and timber would be the best choice. You could make an extremely basic log seat with a plank straddling two uprights, or an equally simple group of 'toadstool' seats. One can envisage the cottager sitting by the back door smoking his pipe on a warm, summer evening, and he was likely to have been sitting on the box that contained logs for the fire — that might give another idea for an occasional seat. For dining, the ideal would be Victorian or Edwardian dining chairs but you could settle for a rustic table of simple planking, with benches.

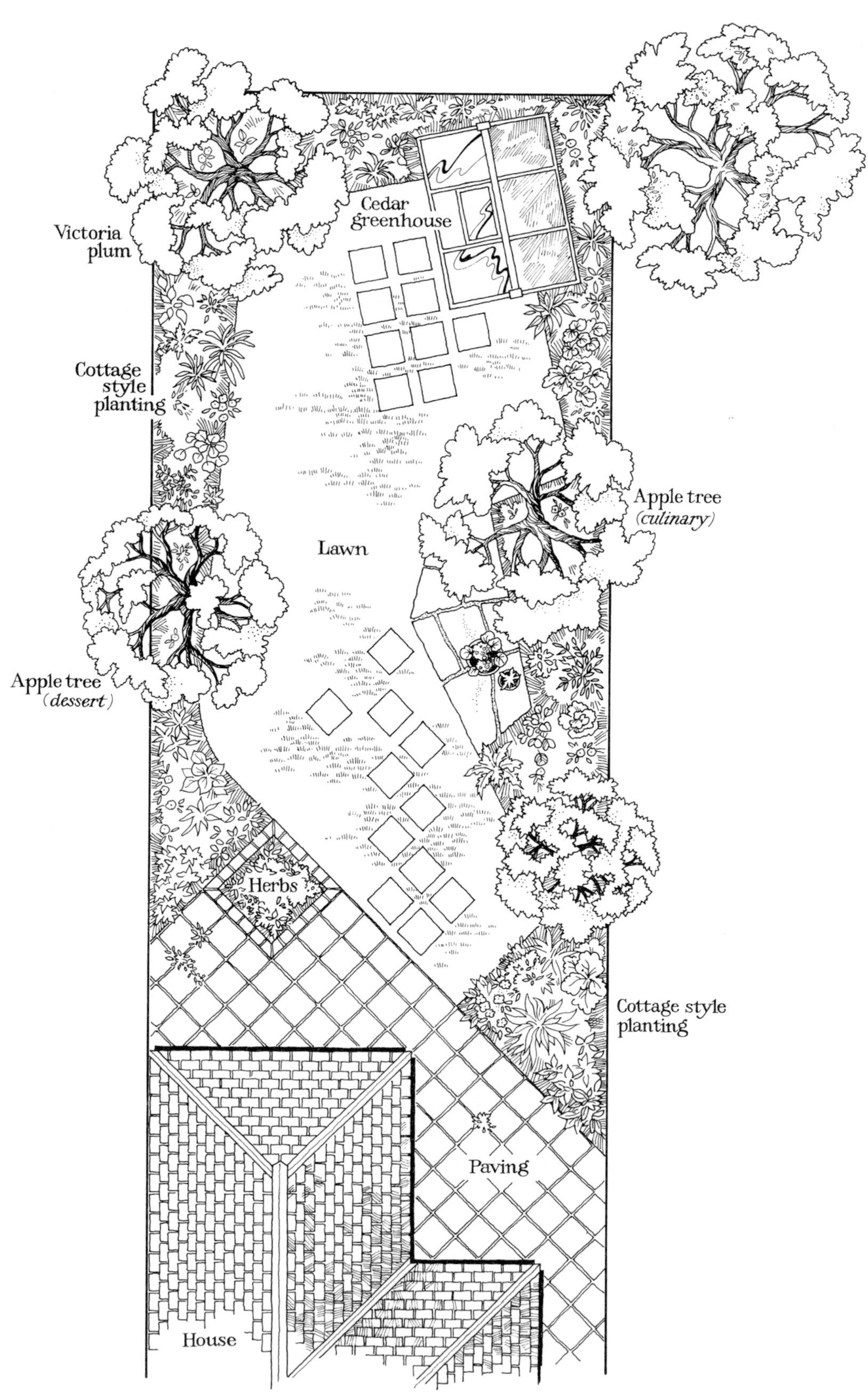
Cedar greenhouse
Victoria plum
Cottage style planting
Apple tree (culinary)
Lawn
Apple tree (dessert)
Herbs
Cottage style planting
Paving
House

Planted pots and ornaments always add the finishing touches to a garden, and a cottage garden is no exception. Clay flower pots are easily available, up to very large sizes suitable for a small tree, and they look most appropriate. Don't forget that half-pots with saucers are perhaps more in scale with colourful fuchsias and geraniums, and strawberry pots can be planted either with the traditional fruit or with ivy or some other suitable trailing plant. Bulbs, too, are good to plant in pots, especially crocus, daffodils and tulips, but it is best to keep them simple and stick to one type of plant per pot.

Position pots on paved areas or shingled areas, beside the back door and even in a plant bed as an occasional feature. On paving, they look attractive when placed as a group of three with, perhaps, one large and two smaller pots, for a sense of balance.

With ornaments there is scope to have a little fun — to use anything that you chance upon that could be in keeping, without looking too contrived and precious. An old coal hod or milk churn could be interesting, and a bird table, bird bath or sundial could look good, as long as you don't clutter the garden with all three in close proximity, and as long as they are simple in shape and style. Again, you want to avoid the gentrified look of a country estate.

Returning for a moment to natural features of the garden, the largest of these is likely to be a tree or trees, and it is at the planning stage that they should be considered, as an integral and important part of the overall design. It is vital to choose a tree that is the appropriate size for the garden, and will not take over as it matures, and, of course, to choose one that is in keeping with the traditional cottage plants.

Cottagers were likely to have a tree in their garden more by accident than design, and it would, of course, have been a native tree. However, many of our most common native trees grow much too large for the average modern garden, so you could settle either for small growers like *Crataegus monogyna*, our native may or hawthorn; an ornamental crab apple such as *Malus* 'John Downie' or for small growing varieties of appropriate trees, such as Kilmarnock willow, *Salix caprea* 'Pendula', or Young's weeping birch, *Betula pendula* 'Youngii'. Fruit trees are, of course, very traditional, and these are considered in greater detail in the chapter devoted to fruit.

When planning the position for a tree, it is essential to allow sufficient distance from the house to accommodate both branches and roots, the latter being particularly important in shrinkable clay soil, where they could cause damage to buildings. It is wise to play safe and plant at a minimum distance of 16 feet (5 m) from the house — more for a larger tree than those mentioned above.

Trees help to attract birds to the garden, but if you want to be more ambitious in the area of livestock, then you need to allow when planning for a beehive or hives, perhaps a chicken run or other appropriate facilities. However, those who prefer to rely on nature to provide wildlife in a garden need not worry unduly, for among the traditional cottage plants are many that will attract birds, bees and butterflies, even in the heart of town.

A design for the small garden of an old or new house, with features to suit the needs of a young family, including a lawn for play and a paved area for sitting and eating outdoors. The cottagey character of this garden is achieved mainly by the borders where traditional plants can be grown

Building the framework

IF YOUR GARDEN HAS an existing framework of an area of paving, a path and screens to the boundary, whether hedges, walls or fences, then you may wish to rely solely on the cottage plants to give the old-fashioned character.

However, if yours is a new plot or you need to carry out alterations to an existing garden that you have inherited, then the work involved in making structural features should be carried out first of all, leaving a basic framework in which the planting can take shape. Of course, you could call in professional help, but you will obviously save money by doing it yourself, and you may find that landscaping your own garden is rewarding, giving a great sense of achievement. Certainly, you will find it more rewarding if you do the job properly, giving a better finish that will last for many years — these are, after all, intended to be permanent features of the garden that do not change from season to season and from year to year, as plants inevitably will.

A good alternative to brick: man-made walling laid in courses has the colour and texture of natural stone

Laying paving

Preparation
Before laying paving, careful consideration should be given to the finished level required. If the paving is to be adjacent to the house it should be laid below the damp proof course. If the paved area is next to a lawn it is convenient to have it on the same level for ease of cutting the grass. For all paved areas, other than paths, there should be a slight slope to ensure that rain water does not collect. This slope should not be less than 2 in (5cm) in every 10 feet (3 m) and should, of course, run away from the house.

Laying the Paving
Mark out the area to be paved with strong lines and pegs. Adjust the tops of the pegs to establish the finished level of the paving.

Excavate this area and refill with 2–3 in (5–7.5 cm) depth of suitable coarse or fine hardcore, thoroughly rammed down to depth of 2½ in (6 cm) below the eventual level and finished with a surface of sand, fine gravel, ash or similar material. Alternatively, especially if used on a domestic driveway, paving may be laid on a 4 in (10 cm) concrete base over 6 in (15 cm) of hardcore.

Make a suitable mix 9:1 clean building sand to cement to produce a stiff but workable mortar which will spread out when a slab is laid on it and pressed down lightly. Only mix enough mortar for half an hour's work.

Starting in the corner of the area use a trowel to place 5 fist-sized dabs of mortar on the foundation — one for each corner and one for the centre of the slab.

Carefully place the slab in position and gently tap it down to the correct level using the trowel or mallet handle.

Slabs may be butted together filling the gaps with a dry sand/cement mix or alternatively a 3/8 in (10 mm) joint recessed by about 1/8 in (3 mm) may be used.

Ensure the slabs are level in the direction at right angles to the slope and that the angle of the slope is consistent. A bulk of timber will help in laying slabs to the right levels.

Cutting
If a paving slab has to be cut, score at the desired position on both sides and edges with a bolster. With the slab on the ground, place the bolster on the score mark and hit firmly until the slab breaks.

Handling
Paving should be handled carefully to avoid damaging edges and faces and stacked on edge on a hard surface.

Paving laid with an irregular edge, phasing into shingle and planting

Building a brick wall

Mortar

Dry ready-mixed mortar (available in 20 kg and 40 kg bags) is easiest to use. A 40 kg bag is normally sufficient to lay 50–60 bricks.

Only mix as much mortar at one time as you can use in an hour. Mortar which has begun to set must be thrown away. Do not add more water.

Foundations

All brickwork needs a firm level foundation from which to build. Soil conditions vary so much in Britain that hard and fast rules for foundations cannot be given. Shrinkable claysoils are particularly troublesome. To be safe, particularly with walls over 3 ft (1 m) high seek the advice of your local building inspector.

Setting out and building foundations

To mark out concrete strip foundations for a wall, set up horizontal profile boards. Stretch lines tied to nails in boards to mark width of trench. On sloping sites, step foundations in multiples of 3 in (75 mm) (brick height).

When the trench is dug, drive timber pegs into the trench bottom so that the tops of each are at the proposed finished foundation level.

Pour in concrete (1 part cement to 5 parts combined aggregate) compacting it with a stout length of timber and tamping it to peg top level. Allow the concrete to harden (7 days).

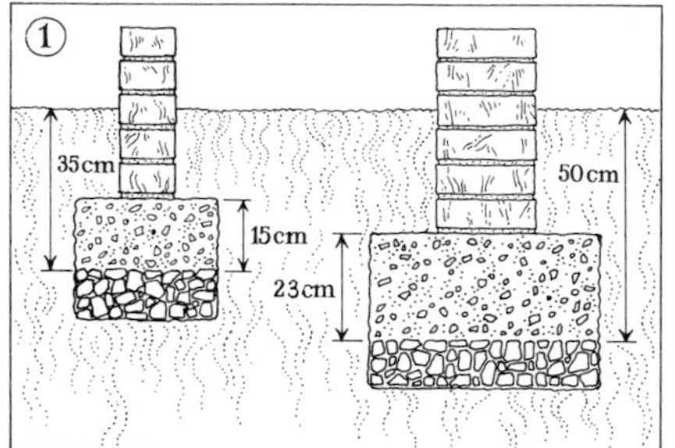

Foundations for half brick wall up to 3 ft (1 m) high.

Foundations for full brick thick wall up to 3 ft (1 m) high.

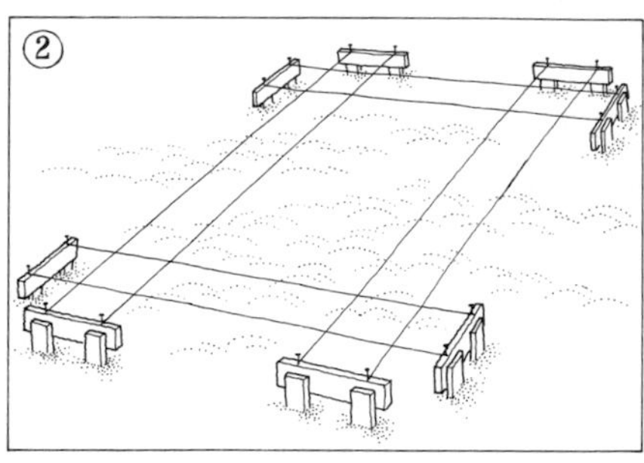

Setting out foundations with profiles.

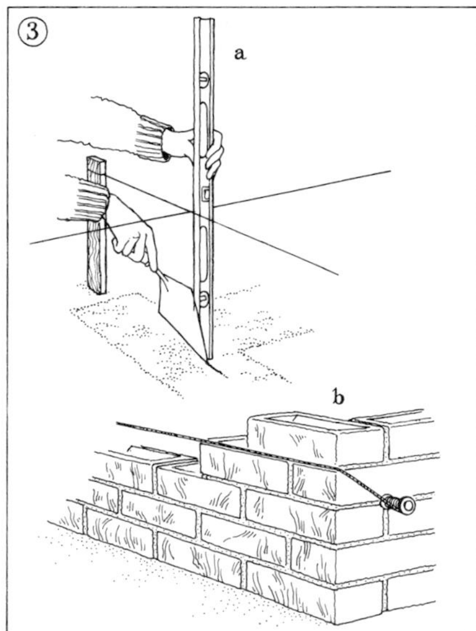

(*above*) Transferring lines from string to mortar.

(*below*) String guide lines.

Setting out and building brickwork

Stretch lines from the profile boards to mark the faces of brick walls.

Lay a screed of mortar on the tops of the foundations. Using a level, transfer lines marked by the string to lines drawn in the mortar.

Remove the strings ready for bricklaying.

Placing bricks carefully along the lines in the mortar, build up the corners of the wall first, to about 6 or 7 courses high, ensuring accuracy with the gauge and level.

When the corners are complete, attach a fine string line with steel pins into each joint in turn to provide a straight, level line along which to set the remaining bricks.

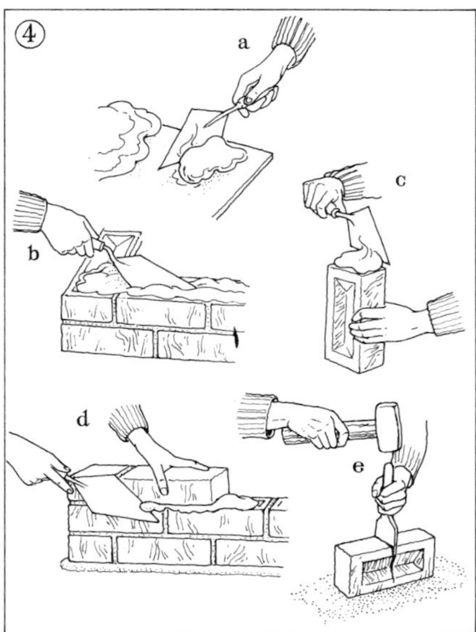

Laying the bricks

Handling a trowel properly is the key to quick bricklaying. You should practise the correct sequence and after a while it will become one smooth operation.

1 Saw off slice of mortar, shape the back into a curve and lift on to trowel with sweeping action.
2 Place the mortar 'sausage' by pulling trowel back and rolling mortar off. Smooth the mortar with the trowel point into a bed ⅜ in (10 mm) thick.
3 To form perpendicular joints butter the end of each brick before laying.

Cutting bricks

Cut bricks on a bed of sand using a bolster and club hammer. If you have many bricks to cut, a simple wooden gauge can be made as a guide.

Making a pond

The most practical material for pool construction is a tough butyl rubber liner. It is simple to use, can be formed into a range of shapes and will last for many years.

Garden centres and water garden specialists will supply to order a liner ready cut to the required size. To calculate the size of liner you need, allow for its length to be the proposed length of the pool plus twice the maximum depth and for the width to be the width of the pool plus twice the maximum depth.

1 Lay a rope or hose to the required shape and size of the pool, adjusting as necessary. Commence digging inside the finished outline.

2 As you dig leave shelves 9 in (23 cm) wide and 9 in (23 cm) below water level to accommodate marginal plants. Excavated soil can be used to create a contour for rock and waterfall if required. Use a spirit level to check that the top edge of the pool is exactly level.

3 Remove any sharp stones or roots from the sides and base of the excavation then spread a layer of sand ½ in (1.25 cm) deep in the bottom, working it into the sides to fill any holes or crevices and leave a smooth lining.

4 Drape the pool liner loosely into the excavation with an even overlap all round. Secure edges with stones or bricks and commence filling with water from the tap.

5 As the pond fills, the stones should be eased off at intervals to allow the liner to fit snugly into the excavation. Some creasing is inevitable, but some creases can be removed by stretching and fitting as the pool fills. When the pool is full the surplus lining can be trimmed off, leaving a 4–5 in (10–12 cm) overlap.

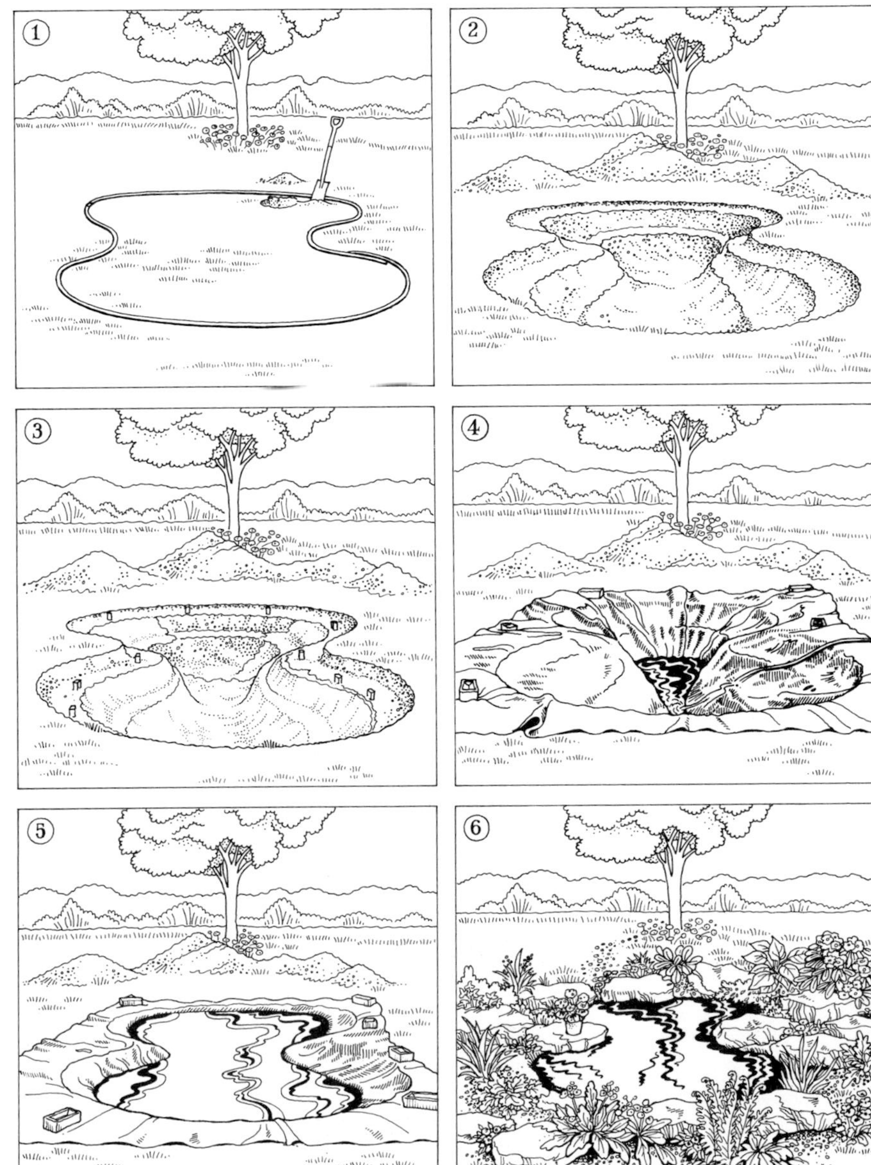

Making a cottage stream

A cottage garden might well have had a stream running through it; this water feature gives the appearance of a natural stream that just happens to meander through your garden, and has been made wider at one point to create a pool. The source of water appears to be a spring which splashes over rocks into the pool, then under a simple stone bridge, and on into a stream which fades out further across the garden.

In fact, the whole feature is made on just the same principle as the garden pond, but has the addition of a rock 'outcrop', and a simple submersible electric pump which continually circulates water over the rocks and back into the pool.

The method of forming the pool and stream is just the same as described for the pond, but the shape will be rather like a tadpole, as the pond narrows into the curved stream. Our first garden design gives an idea for the actual outline of the feature, but this can, if necessary, be adjusted to suit the individual site. The outline should be slightly irregular to give a look of natural informality, but avoid a fussy 'scalloped' line as this would not only look unnatural, but would create practical problems.

When the butyl liner is in place, rocks should be positioned to form the outcrop. Choose a few pieces of good size, for a fiddly look should be avoided, and combine them with smaller rock chippings in order to give

A large piece of rock with a natural arch makes a simple bridge over the stream bed, which is surrounded by dense planting

Irregular sized pieces of York stone laid to create an informal ground pattern and interplanted with alyssum

Steps laid in a sweeping curve beside a bank of Polygonum, *which although not strictly a cottage plant, has a nice soft look* en masse

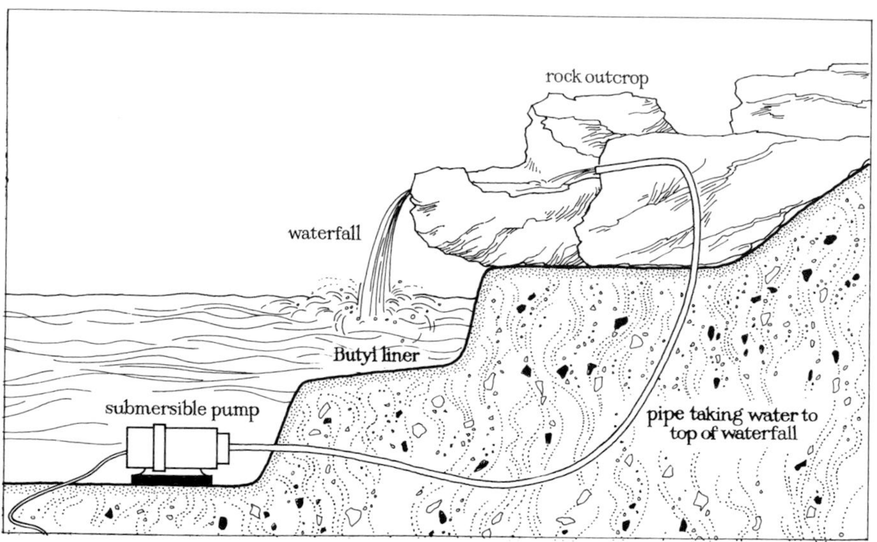

the impression of a natural feature that phases into its surroundings. Each piece of rock will probably have at least one 'face' that looks weathered and mature. If it has been blasted from a quarry the other surfaces might look quite new. Position the rock so that the mature face is showing — moss on the surface adds even more character — and try to keep continuity in the strata; the natural 'grain' of the rock should run horizontally on every piece.

The height of the rock outcrop should be not more than 2–3 feet (60–90 cm), and the rocks should be tilted slightly backwards, so that they lie into the bank, rather than appearing to be perched on the edge of the pond. As you position the rock, build in a length of hosepipe, as shown, camouflaging it as you proceed.

This will then be ready for connection to an electric submersible pump positioned on the bed of the pool. The pump and accessories are available from garden centres and water garden specialists in the form of a waterfall kit. Once it is in position, the pump is powered by connection to an ordinary 13 amp three pin socket via a transformer, which reduces the power to a very low voltage for safety and economy of use.

All in all, an intriguing way of using modern materials and equipment to create a traditional feature of natural appearance.

Preparing the soil for plants

The majority of the cottage plants will settle themselves in the garden and remain there for several years. Certainly you are likely to move some, to add new clumps and cuttings and to sow or plant annual flowers each year in accessible places, but in general all the plants are intended to grow together in a happy profusion, and if they are to remain happy in the long term then it is essential to give them a good start by thoroughly preparing the soil, for a little extra effort now will really pay dividends later.

The ideal soil is a perfect balance of humus (the dark, crumbly substance that results from thousands of years of decay of plant and animal life), sand, clay and chalk, but many soils have a deficiency or excess of one or more of these elements.

Clay soil is heavy and is often wet and cold in autumn and winter, or hard and cracked in summer. Roots often cannot penetrate the soil, and many plants do not thrive. This can be improved by the addition of an organic material such as peat, well rotted manure or vegetable compost, which help to create humus, and sharp sand to improve drainage, making the soil more porous.

Both sandy and chalky soils will also benefit from the addition of organic material, which should be incorporated into the soil as you dig it over before planting. However, before you can dig, you should clear the soil of any stones, brickbats or other rubbish and also clear it of perennial weeds. This is a tiresome job, but is well worth the initial effort, for if left undisturbed such weeds will be a terrible nuisance every year.

Where the soil is in reasonable condition and is fairly loose and crumbly, it is sufficient to turn it over to the depth of one spade (known as single digging), but problem soils will really benefit from double digging — being turned over to a greater depth. Beneath the first spade's depth you will probably find the subsoil, which should always be kept separate from the topsoil. Loosen it with a fork, making it more crumbly and penetrable, and then replace the topsoil incorporating organic material, as described. All soils will also benefit from the addition of bonemeal or a general fertilizer in granular form to get plants going with a flourish.

Selecting cottage garden plants

WHILST IT IS IMPORTANT to create an appropriate framework for a cottage garden, using materials that are sympathetic to its style and mood and employing them in a manner not too far removed from the time-honoured way in which cottagers might have done, the vital elements that will finally identify your garden as being in the authentic style of the English country cottage are the plants.

If, when you have done the ground work of planning and shaping the garden, it still looks fairly nondescript, do not despair, for once you start to introduce cottage garden plants you will find that they complete the job for

An informal mixture of plants

Authentic cottage garden plants capture a period atmosphere

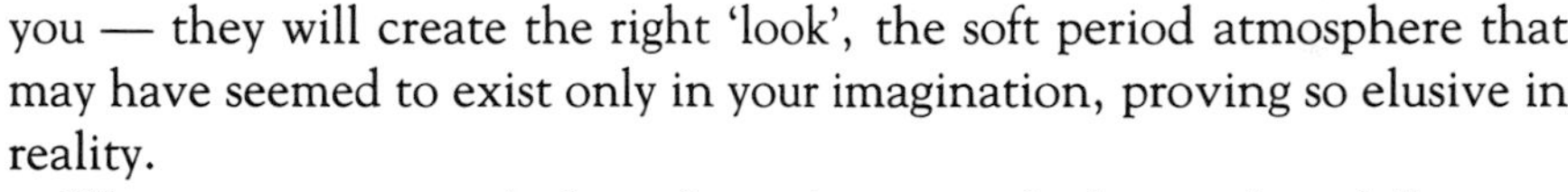

you — they will create the right 'look', the soft period atmosphere that may have seemed to exist only in your imagination, proving so elusive in reality.

We cannot pretend that the selection of plants that follows is necessarily comprehensive; it would probably be almost impossible to compile the definitive list of cottage garden plants. By the same token, we may have included a few recommendations that would cause more knowledgeable horticulturists to raise their eyebrows. If so, it is often because, when composing our own cottage garden, we found them so useful for some characteristic of flower or form (usually the latter).

Glory of the Snow

The plants that we have finally included satisfy, to the best of our knowledge, two basic criteria — firstly, they are authentic cottage garden plants, and secondly, but equally importantly, every one is available commercially. There are few things more frustrating to a gardener than to hear of or read about a plant that captures the imagination, only to discover it cannot be obtained for love nor money. The *raison d'etre* of our garden and subsequently this book, was, after all, to prove that the cottage garden is still relevant and can still be created by town and country dwellers alike.

Some of the plants mentioned are freely available from many garden centres and retail nurseries who carry a regular, but fairly comprehensive range of trees, shrubs, herbaceous plants and bulbs; or can be grown from seed that is invariably found in the flower packet range carried not only by garden centres and shops, but also by chain stores and supermarkets. Some less common plants may be available as shrubs, roots, bulbs or seed only from more specialist firms who supply by mail order and for these the list of suppliers at the back of the book will prove helpful. The plant check-lists also give ready reference for selection.

Although some of the old-fashioned plants may no longer be available commercially, others have been the subject of breeding and hybridization, so that their families have expanded to include offspring that were not even thought of by the cottage gardener in, say, Victorian times. Some cultivars have been produced to bring new colours, others to be more manageable as garden plants and still others more resistant to pests and diseases.

These have given us food for thought, but we have firmly decided to recommend varieties that maintain the spirit of the old plants — for instance, we believe that if you are to grow delphiniums in a cottage garden, then they should be blue. However, we have not been so purist as to exclude cultivars that have practical advantages and improved characteristics, just because they are twentieth century introductions. So, delphiniums might be blue, but we have not scorned the shorter, sturdier cultivars that do not need staking, recognizing that they have value in a modern garden and some gardeners may prefer them to their less easily controlled forebears.

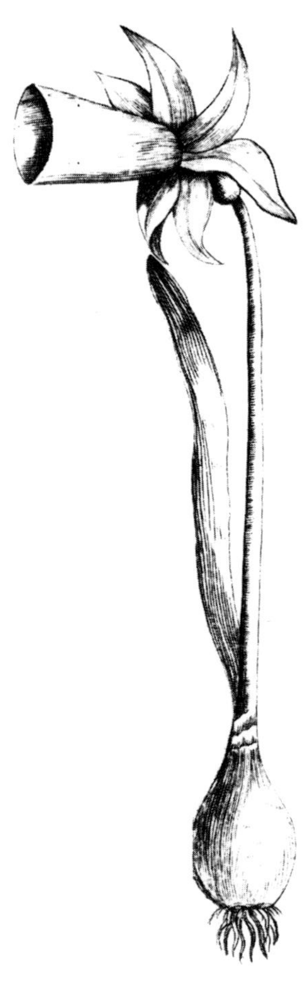

Advances in breeding are particularly noticeable where roses are concerned; most of the oldest varieties, although lovely and often steeped in history and tradition, flowered once in the year and were soon over. Newer varieties are repeat flowering and we have come to value roses in our gardens for the show of colour they give all through the summer and even into autumn. Fortunately for the cottage gardener, some of the newer shrub roses are not only resistant to disease, but have much of the softness of form, flower shape and colour — and often much of the perfume — of the older favourites, so we have tried to combine the best of both worlds in our recommendations.

The style of planting traditional to cottage gardens makes it almost impossible to devise a set planting plan. Cottagers would probably have scorned such an idea anyway, relying on their instinct, taste and eye for colour and composition. Nevertheless, it is useful to work within a framework of guidelines dictated more by commonsense and practical possibilities than by any desire to be dogmatic.

The first general principle is the mixture of plants. Almost uniquely, cottage gardens depend equally for their effect on representatives from virtually every group of garden plants with which we are familiar. There should be hardy perennials, of course, for they include some of the most familiar plants of the English countryside; but there should also be annual and biennial flowers; shrubs, including shrub and species roses; climbers; bulbs that will naturalize as part of the permanent planting; herbs that were used for both culinary and medicinal purposes; fruit, which would be grown not in its own plot, but amongst the ornamental flowers and

possibly vegetables. The aim should not be to give every group its own allotted space in the garden, but to create an exuberant mixture where each is rubbing shoulders with the other.

As for the arrangement of plants, obviously it is sensible to start with a framework of larger subjects, both as a backdrop around the perimeter of the garden and as highpoints within the plot. Shrubs and roses will be particularly useful here for bulk, climbers as a tall, softening framework and the taller perennials and biennials like hollyhocks, foxgloves and delphiniums as occasional colourful punctuations, thus avoiding any tendency to flatness or uniformity in the larger planted areas of the garden.

Those plants which might be termed as medium-sized will come next, taking up the middle ground and stepping down towards the centre of the garden perhaps, or towards the front of a border, a path or the edge of an area of paving. Along such edges and in the foreground of the plant areas the multitude of low-growing and creeping plants will fuzz and blur, their dainty character adding essential softness and charm.

You would probably want to plant the larger shrubs and roses as individual specimens, partly because of the particular restrictions of space, but also in order to appreciate to the full the beauty of their shape and outline. However, with the medium-sized plants and low growers (and almost all perennials, bulbs and annuals, regardless of size) single plants will look scrappy and unsatisfying. It is better to plant in groups of three, five, seven or even more, depending on the ultimate size of the plants and the amount of space you want them to fill.

The ideal overall impression should be that of a dense profusion of plants associating informally with each other and offering interest all through the year. The cottage plants are interdependent for their effect, softly flowing and merging with each other. There is no place here for regimentation or formality.

Although it is impossible to give a rigid planting guide, some plants are obviously happiest in certain positions and their preferences should, of course, be taken into account. Also, there is a subtle difference between happy profusion and an ugly, clogged mass of plants that have been given insufficient space to grow, so it is advisable to give new plants some room for manoeuvre and show off the full attractions of their form.

When selecting and planting, you need also to be aware of the distinction between, say, summer flowering perennials that will have nothing to show in the colder months; shrubs that are deciduous, but may have berries or fruits and twigs for autumn interest; climbers and shrubs that are evergreen and can be at their most interesting in winter months. The secret is to combine all of these so that the garden is never dull. Although it is obviously during spring and summer that a cottage garden is at its most colourful, perfumed and charming, the snowdrops and primroses of early spring should not be forgotten, nor Michaelmas daisies in autumn and traditional holly and ivy at Christmas time.

If you are new to gardening or unsure of your ability to compose a harmonious collection of plants, there is no need to worry that all this advice means that cottage gardening demands a high level of skill and knowledge, or that it is desirable to try and grow all the many plants that might have been found in cottage gardens. Rather, have the confidence to select your own favourites and let your own ideas show through; as long as you reject rigid planting designs in favour of cheerful informality and as long as you are working with the authentic cottage plants, then almost anything goes. In gardening, even if we do make mistakes, nature is usually kind enough to allow us another chance — a new season, a new year in which to change our mind or put things right.

Yet another reason for the uselessness of giving formal planting plans is the simple fact that, just as today, no two cottage gardens can ever have looked exactly alike. Some were more densely planted than others; some were much flatter in appearance than the kind of planting that we have

Dense planting which combines bolder shrubs with annuals and perennials

'Minna' by Helen Allingham — a charming inspiration for cottage gardeners today

advocated, but were no less authentically cottagey for that. They simply seem to be framed in climbers and taller growing plants, but within the garden itself to consist largely of spreading subjects and low-growing flowers like pinks and pansies.

Yet other cottage gardens reflected the poverty and need against which their owners struggled, their few flowers like occasional rays of sunshine on a dull, grey day — the dullness consisting mostly of half starved vegetables and a skinny hen to match.

Without wishing to indulge in lofty moral sentiments we have found, nonetheless, that it is virtually impossible to dissociate the cottage plants from the people who grew them, from the way of life that they and their children knew, both in the country and in cities. Making a cottage garden now is not just an exercise in growing pretty flowers; it is also surely an acknowledgement that the values and traditions of their humble way of life may have been poor in material terms, but were rich in human terms. It is in their lives that the history of our nation is embodied just as much as in the actions of monarchs and politicians and the people of power.

Shrubs

A NUMBER OF SHRUBS have an important and rightful place in the line-up of cottage garden plants, so they can happily be included in a garden in the cottage style and look very much in keeping.

Fortunately for the modern cottage gardener, most of the traditional shrubs are both attractive and extremely useful in their own right. In return for very little attention, they will oblige with robust, woody growth, in time filling quite a space and their permanence of character and appearance can help to hold together visually groups of softer, more wayward plants. They are useful, too, in providing 'bulk' — to fill a bare corner or grow against a wall or fence — and to create a substantial lasting backdrop for plants of a more ephemeral nature.

In this respect, the particular usefulness of evergreens is obvious; they provide interest and foliage colour — possibly colour from berries, too — during the cold, dull winter months when the choice of flowering plants is much more limited and their special value cannot be underrated. There are, too, several deciduous shrubs without which a cottage garden would hardly be complete — lilac, mock orange blossom, flowering currant, rose of Sharon, snowberry, — to give them their common, old-fashioned names — and of course roses, to which a separate chapter is devoted.

A word, here, about the way in which shrubs can and should be used in a cottage garden — or firstly about how they should not be used, for the principle of mixed planting should always prevail and that rules out such modern concepts as a shrub border or — worse still in this context — a bed of conifers and heathers in the style that has become popular in recent years. Certainly such features are attractive in their own right and in the right style of garden, but they are altogether too stiffly composed for the informal hurly-burly of the cottage garden.

Rather than being planted in large groups of formal beds, the shrubs in a cottage garden should occur at strategic intervals; larger specimens can be planted individually, as background or screening plants as described. Lower growing shrubs could be planted in a group of three or five, or in an informal drift (especially appropriate for ground cover shrubs) but as a general rule, all shrubs should be combined with other plants —

surrounded by perennials, perhaps, or underplanted with bulbs or annuals. In this way, they can best fulfil their usefulness as linch-pins amidst a profusion of plants of softer, seasonal beauty.

This is not to say that a shrub of splendid size and graceful shape should be surrounded by plants that blur its attractive outline and waste its potential. It would be a pity to obscure the beauty of form of a single specimen of one of the traditional cottage evergreens like yew, holly, bay or box. All of these need to be given a little space and would, perhaps, be best complemented by low underplanting.

Taxus baccata, the common or English yew, can be regarded as a large shrub or small to medium-sized tree. It is one of the very few conifers native to Britain and is happy growing in most conditions — even in deep shade or on chalky soils, although it needs good drainage. However, in spite of its adaptability and value as a garden plant, the yew has traditionally been regarded with some suspicion and foreboding. Its association with churchyards, where it is so often to be found, is one obvious reason and so, presumably, is its poisonous seed.

Even these reasons seem barely to account for the stories about yew that, according to Gerard, abounded in the sixteenth century and before. He recounts them vigorously, writing, 'The Yew Tree, as Galen reporteth, is of a venomous quality and against man's nature.' It was widely believed that if birds ate the fruit their feathers would fall out and that sickness, and even death, would come to anyone who slept under the shadow of the tree. However, we can be heartened by Gerard's cheerful good sense in assuring us that as a schoolboy, he and his friends slept not only in its shadow, but even in its branches without coming to any harm.

Perhaps the dark green leaves, which look almost black *en masse*, contribute to the sinister characteristics attributed to very old, larger trees, but as a feature of the cottage garden, a plant of moderate size can be a useful focal point throughout the year and a foil for brighter colours. There are numerous forms of *Taxus baccata*, but to be truly cottagey, we feel that it is best to keep to those with the familiar dark green foliage and especially either English yew or the columnar Irish yew, *Taxus baccata* 'Fastigiata'.

Equally traditional, but with happier associations, is holly. The very word sounds cheerful and as John Clare reminds us, for the cottager it was an intrinsic part of the Christmas cheer and celebrations which, for a time at least, lightened the cares of poverty and need:

> Christmas is come and every hearth
> Makes room to give him welcome now
> Een want will dry its tears in mirth
> And crown him wi a holly bough.

Ilex aquifolium, the common holly, is a superb shrub or small tree. In common with so many cottage garden plants, it is native, easy to grow and unfussy as to position or soil; because of this, it is especially useful in city or coastal gardens and can make an attractive hedge.

The beauty and appeal of the long-lasting, bright red berries, which are borne on the female plants, are familiar and it is always disappointing

Chaenomeles (commonly known as japonica) is useful in an upright position or against a wall

Rhododendron *'Pink Pearl'*

when the season for holly berries is poor. Female plants must obviously be pollinated by male forms, but there is one particularly notable self-fertile holly, *Ilex aquifolium* 'Pyramidalis', which, as its name suggests, has a conical shape, especially when young, and handsome bright green leaves.

There are, in fact, very many cultivars and clones of *Ilex aquifolium*; to be strictly authentic, the common holly with plain, dark green leaves is most traditional, but really almost any cultivar would be in keeping in a cottage garden. The small hedgehog holly, *Ilex a.* 'Ferox', for instance, has been known at least since the early seventeenth century. In a garden of reasonable size, you might consider growing one silver and one golden variegated holly, as well as one specimen of familiar plain green. Although holly is quite slow growing, if plants should become too large they can be trimmed or even cut back hard without adverse effect and hedges can, of course, be clipped, although it is advisable to wear stout gardening gloves for protection!

Another traditional plant that can be clipped to excellent effect is box. The common box, *Buxus sempervirens*, is again a large shrub or small tree, but is much slower growing even than holly and less common. Box is widely associated with formal gardens, where it was often used as a neatly clipped hedge or low edging to a knot garden or herb garden. Although such trim formality is hardly in keeping with the cottage style, box should certainly not be entirely overlooked. It is a most attractive plant, with its small, densely packed leaves, like shiny green leather, and is certainly appropriate in a cottage garden as an individual specimen, which can be allowed to grow eventually into a small tree. Box could also be grown in a simple clay flower pot of suitable size and clipped to form a pyramid — indeed, it is in pyramid form that plants are most likely to be found in

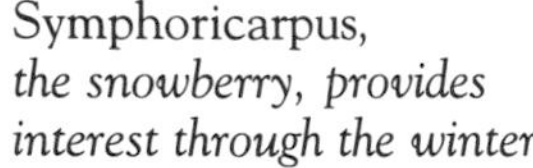

Symphoricarpus, *the snowberry, provides interest through the winter*

Syringa vulgaris — *the common lilac*

garden centres, although their price reflects the length of time needed to produce a well-shaped specimen. If grown in a pot, (two specimens could be grown as a pair in pots on either side of a door or gate), the plant should, of course, be watered as necessary and given fertilizer during spring and summer. In the garden, box is unfussy as to position and soil.

Of similar character to box is the bay tree, *Laurus nobilis*. Although often associated with more formal use in town gardens, it too can find a place in a cottage garden, and was traditionally used for many purposes beyond the familiar flavouring of the dried leaves for stews and casseroles. Indeed, John Parkinson wrote poetically of bay, 'From the cradle to the grave we have still use of it, we have still need of it,' explaining that the leaves were used for bathing wounded limbs and to make a drink to ease the stomach, as well as to season pots in which meat and drink were preserved. They were fashioned into crowns for the heads of the living and used to adorn the bodies of the dead.

Bay is a tender plant and should therefore be grown in a warm, sheltered spot or given protection in winter. Good sized plants are expensive to buy, especially the ball bays with mop heads on tall stems, but this need not deter the cottage gardener, because like box, a pyramid bay would be much more appropriate.

The choice, glossy foliage of holly and bay brings to mind the equally choice evergreen foliage of rhododendron, but here there is a note of controversy, because not all horticulturists are agreed that rhododendrons are necessarily cottage garden plants. It is felt that they came too late to this country, that their appearance is too grand, showy and aristocratic. Perhaps this is a valid argument, but within the restrictions of certain varieties, we tend to side with those who would allow this shrub a place in a cottage garden — not least because of the usefulness of its dense evergreen growth and bulky, rounded form.

Of course, the major practical consideration is that being ericaceous, rhododendrons are lime-hating and therefore prefer a light, sandy or peaty soil. However, where conditions are suitable, they will flourish helpfully in shade and reward the gardener with those magnificent flowers. As to varieties, it is obviously necessary in a small garden to avoid those that make huge, rambling plants and, in the spirit of the cottage garden, advisable to avoid flashy colours that are out of keeping.

Our advice would be to choose compact growers with soft pink or mauve blooms — such as *R.* 'Blue Diamond', 'Bluebird' and 'Pink Drift'. When there is space for a larger plant, (6 × 4 feet/2 × 1·2 m) it is hard to beat that all time favourite 'Pink Pearl' or the lovely pale bluish mauve 'Fastuosum Flore Pleno'.

The advantages of bulk and a large bloom are offered, too, by hydrangeas. Again, some caution is perhaps necessary to maintain the cottagey character of planting; the brighter shades of blue and pink hydrangeas are definitely too vivid, too sulphurous for the softness of colour of most traditional cottage plants and those huge flower heads can be too heavy and overpowering against their daintiness. The best solution is, we feel, not to reject hydrangeas altogether, but to choose the lacecaps, which bear a head of dense fertile flowers surrounded by sterile florets. The effect is of a Victorian doyley or lace trimmed bonnet — quite delightful. The varieties 'White Wave' and 'Veitchii' are especially to be recommended for their hardiness, free flowering and soft colouring.

With hydrangeas, we have moved on to deciduous shrubs appropriate for the modern cottage garden. Of these, the taller characters are all ideal for softening corners or against a wall or fence — shrubs such as chaenomeles, *Kerria japonica*, philadelphus, symphoricarpos, syringa. If just one each of these were planted in a medium-sized garden, they would create the framework of the authentic cottage style, as well as providing a delightful range of flowers or berries through many months of the year.

We'll gather lilacs in the
spring again,
We'll walk together down an
English lane.

Lilac (*Syringa vulgaris*) was traditionally known as blue pipe, but the familiar modern name is much more evocative and appropriate for this beautiful shrub with its full, generous clusters of deliciously perfumed blooms, contrasting effectively with the soft green leaves which curl and wrinkle at the edges.

The common lilac is a large, vigorous shrub, which throws up suckers from the roots; it thrives in most soils, especially chalky ones and prefers full sun, flowering in May–June. The species itself has blooms of the familiar lilac colour, but it has given rise to more cultivars than almost any other garden shrub, with flowers ranging in colour from deep purple and every shade of mauve to deep red, carmine, rose pink and white or yellow. It seems to us that in a cottage garden, lilac should be lilac, although soft white would not be inappropriate. Certainly, *Syringa vulgaris* 'Alba' has long been cultivated and there is something delightfully evocative of lace tablecloths and old-fashioned weddings about white lilac.

St Johns Wort

The sweet white flowers of philadelphus or mock orange blossom are also traditionally associated with brides — a fact perhaps reflected in names like 'Virginal' and 'Innocence', given to cultivars introduced early this century when such associations were probably more appropriate!

In the sixteenth century, both Gerard and Parkinson refer to philadelphus as a white lilac, but it was already known in single and double forms. They actually call it white pipe, a reference to the fact that when the pith is removed from the stalks and branches, they are hollow like a pipe.

The great appeal of philadelphus lies not only in the delicate appearance of the clustered white blossom, but also in its heady fragrance, and it is just that fragrance which seems to have greatly disturbed poor Gerard, who wrote of the flowers, 'in my judgement they are too sweet, troubling and molesting the head in a very strange manner. I once gathered the floures and layed them in my chamber window, which smelled more strongly after they had lien together a few houres, with such an unacquainted savor that they awaked me out of sleep, so that I could not rest till I had cast them out of my chamber.'

That combination of a simple, yet deeply scented flower, borne lightly on a robust woody plant that thrives even in poor soils, makes philadelphus an ideal cottage garden plant. Again, there are numerous hybrids and cultivars, but in this case, almost any would be at home in a cottage garden. However, particularly to be recommended (and easily available) are *Philadelphus coronarius* 'Aureus', a form of the most commonly cultivated species which has leaves that are a lovely light, bright yellow when young, turning greenish-yellow later, *Philadelphus* 'Belle Etoile' and the dwarf, compact *P.* 'Manteau d'Hermine', which has double, creamy-white flowers. All are strongly scented.

What a night the wind howls hisses and but stops
To howl more loud while the snow volly keeps
Insessant batter at the window pane
Making our comfort feel as sweet again
And in the morning when the tempest drops
At every cottage door mountainous heaps
Of snow lies drifted that all entrance stops
Untill the beesom and the shovel gains
The path — and leaves a wall on either side.
'Snow Storm' by John Clare

Symphoricarpus rivularis, the snowberry, is renowned, as its name suggests, not for its flowers but for its abundant display of milky white berries like huge pearls, which appear in autumn and last on the plant well into the season of winter frost and snow. Another obliging shrub, snowberry will grow in all types of soil and even flourishes in the shade or under the dripping branches of a large tree. It sends out suckers from the base, which help the plant to increase quite rapidly in width, making dense thickets of upright stems. This means that, in common with lilac and philadelphus, it benefits from being cleared of the mass of old, scruffy twiggy growth that accumulates at its base.

Also of suckering habit and tall growth is *Kerria japonica.* In April and May its slender, gracefully arching branches are covered in single yellow flowers and after the leaves have fallen, the stems are a fresh, attractive green. Kerria is especially useful against a wall or fence, where in true cottage style it will often assert its free spirit by quickly outstripping the height of the wall, the ends of its branches waving gently to passers-by.

Two excellent shrubs for a modern cottage garden are deutzia and ribes, the flowering currant. Not only are these plants readily available from nurseries and garden centres, but because most cultivars blend well with

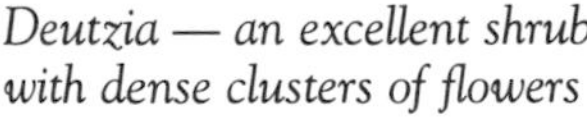

Deutzia — an excellent shrub with dense clusters of flowers

Vinca minor — *the periwinkle*

cottage planting, they offer flexibility of choice according to need and space available. If a tall, robust shrub is required then *Deutzia* 'Mont Rose' will bear its dense clusters of mauvy-pink flowers to a height of about 6 feet (2 m). Similarly, *Ribes* 'Pulborough Scarlet' is a fast, vigorous grower and excellent for a quick effect. Amongst the lower growing cultivars, *Deutzia x rosea* grows less than 3 feet (1 m) tall and bears lovely delicate pink blooms. Its graceful, arching branches are quite open and do need room to spread for the plant to express its full beauty, so sufficient space should be allowed when planting. *Ribes sanguineum* 'Brocklebankii' is a bushy plant about 3 feet (1 m) tall, which has pale pink flowers and appreciates some shade.

Still lower growing and perhaps the plant that above all epitomizes balmy bee-filled summer afternoons in the country is lavender. It is probably the association with lavender water, pot-pourri, elderly ladies and scented pillows and sachets that makes lavender such a distinctly old-fashioned plant, yet still so evocative and appealing. Its uses certainly go back a very long way and not only as a perfume. Gerard recommends that lavender water should be smelt or dabbed on the temples and forehead as a relief for headaches and also says that dried powdered lavender flowers mixed with cinnamon, nutmeg and cloves and diluted in lavender water, 'doth help the panting and passion of the heart, prevaileth against giddinesse, turning or swimming of the braine, and members subject to the palsie.'

Today, lavender is grown commercially, especially in Norfolk, for its oil and dried flowers and is even used by one imaginative chef as the basis for a sorbet.

Lavandula spica or spike lavender is the traditional old English lavender and there are several forms available. The oldest and most cottagey are probably two that make rather nice compact plants — 'Munstead' and the wonderfully named 'Twickel Purple'. Lavender is extremely useful as a garden plant in hot, dry spots, where it will flower from July through to September; bear the low growers in mind as a soft grey-blue cloud of charming and sometimes slightly untidy growth for the front of a bed or as edging along a path. If they should become a little unruly, making the path difficult to negotiate, then the plants can simply be cut with shears after they have finished flowering.

Lavender blue often combines well in nature with sunshine yellow and there are two yellow-flowered cottage shrubs which should definitely not be forgotten. The first is broom and here some clarification is needed, for there are two distinct, but closely allied, genuses of shrubs — cytisus, the common broom and genista, some of whose species are referred to as various types of broom, although the most common is *Genista hispanica*, Spanish gorse, the prickly mounds so frequently seen on sunny banks and open spaces.

Both are natives of southern Europe and have long been familiar in Britain, but for a cottage garden, cytisus is much the most attractive and useful plant. It seems that this was the broom to which Gerard was

Kolkwitzia amabilis, *not strictly authentic but with the characteristics of a cottage shrub*

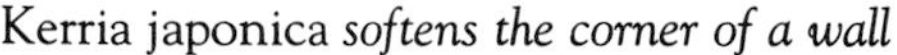

Kerria japonica *softens the corner of a wall*

Broom

referring when he tells us that as the mass of small, yellow pea-like flowers appeared in late April–May, the young buds were gathered and laid in pickle or salt and later washed or boiled to be used in salads 'as Capers be, and be eaten with no less delight.' He also confides the information that Henry VIII was wont to drink the distilled water of broom flowers 'against surfets and diseases thereof arising.' Hardly a good advertisement, on consideration, for its efficacy!

Our favourite broom, and we feel the best for a small garden in cottage style, is *Cytisus praecox*, either the yellow 'Allgold' or the soft, opaque white flowered 'Albus'. Both are quite small shrubs, but although they do not grow to more than 2 or 3 feet (60–90 cm) tall, their arching branches bear elegantly massed sprays of bloom from the base of the plant. This soft, curving shape makes cytisus useful at the corner of a sunny wall, breaking its angled line, or similarly to soften a group of plants of stiffer habit, its branches seeming to reach outward into the garden.

Rose of Sharon or St John's wort (*Hypericum calycinum*) is an evergreen ground cover plant that is ideal for dry places, even in shade. It is a robust grower and can become invasive like a weed, but you feel you could forgive it anything for those bright, sunshine yellow flowers which turn their fluffy, red-tinged faces to the sun in such an appealing way.

Gerard, too, was very keen on the plant, but in this case for its ability to heal deep wounds, even those that went through the body or were made with a poisoned weapon. For this purpose, he passes on to us his recipe in every detail:

> Take white wine two pintes, oile olive foure pounds, oile of Turpentine two pounds, the leaves, floures, and seeds of St Johns Wort of each two great handfulls gently bruised; put them all together into a great double glasse, and set it in the sun eight to ten daies; then boile them in the same glass per Balneum Marie, that is, in a kettle of water, with some straw in the bottome, wherein the glass must stand to boil; which done, strain the liquor from the herbs, and do as you did before, putting in the like quantity of herbs, floures and seeds, but not any more wine.

This, he tells us ominously, makes an oil the colour of blood.

Another useful and evocative plant is periwinkle (*Vinca minor*). The name seems so appropriate for the simple, shy, unassuming little flowers of clear blue, dotting the surface of the matted evergreen leaves. The stems of periwinkle are long, slender and trailing, making it almost more a perennial than a shrub, and the plants spread quickly and obligingly to give really effective ground cover under trees and larger shrubs.

Obliging is a description that could apply equally to fuchsias. The Victorians would have grown showy tender fuchsias, both in the garden and on the window-sill, but we are thinking here of the hardy shrubs — especially *Fuchsia* 'Riccartonii' — that thrive year after year, in sun or shade and even in seaside conditions. We have especially fond and vivid memories of a brilliant summer's day on the Isle of Man, where fuchsias grew wild and were covered in long, scarlet flowers like clusters of rubies dangling, dazzling by the roadside.

If you are unfamiliar with fuchsia as a shrub, do not be deceived by those neat little pot plants into imagining that 'Riccartonii' is a low, compact plant, for it will reach up to 6 feet (2 m) in height and about 4 feet (1.2 m) across in time. The mass of dangling blooms give it a distinctly cottagey feel and the colour — strong without being gaudy — can be useful in late summer. However, if you don't have room for such a large shrub, do not despair, for *Fuchsia* 'Tom Thumb' is true to its name, reaching only just over a foot (30 cm) tall, but bearing in profusion scarlet and violet blooms.

It seems to us that fuchsias are not always as appreciated as shrubs as they might be. Some are more hardy than others, but even the slightly tender souls, if cut down by winter frosts, will rise again in spring and they are such graceful, well-shaped plants that combine happily with the simple annuals of summer, especially with soft pink or white flowers like stocks and alyssum and even with the blue of periwinkle or the paler shades of *Campanula carpatica*, with its open, cup-shaped blooms.

This, then, is a selection of many of the shrubs that are not only authentic cottage garden plants, but are still easily available from nurseries and garden centres. It is well worth perusing catalogues and plant display areas before you buy, but it is possible to become waylaid and even rather bogged down by a tantalizing description or a plant that happens to be in bloom when you see it. The excitement and enjoyment of planning can be lost if you have too rigid a plant schedule that proves difficult to fill, but to achieve and maintain the character of a cottage garden, it is as well to be fairly single-minded when choosing your shrubs.

If bought from a garden centre, shrubs are likely to be container grown, in which case the plant itself should be well shaped and look healthy, with good colour in the leaves; it should also be well established in the container and not come easily away from the soil as soon as you start to pick it up gently by the stem. The soil itself should be moist and not appear to have been allowed to dry out and bake hard.

Container grown shrubs can be planted at any time of year, except when the ground is waterlogged or frozen. Bare root shrubs, which are often supplied as mail order plants, are lifted straight from the ground in which they have been grown and their planting season is from October to March although, again, not when the soil is waterlogged or frozen. The plants should, if it proves necessary, be stored until planted in a cool, airy shed or garage.

If you are new to gardening, reputable garden retailers will supply detailed information on how to plant shrubs, whether container grown or open-ground, and most offer a guarantee, provided the plant has been properly treated and cared for. More experienced gardeners will know that many of the cottage garden shrubs can easily be propagated from cuttings taken from established plants in the gardens of friends or relatives (not, please, from parks or gardens open to the public!) — an activity that is not only satisfying and rewarding for its own sake, but that, with its 'something from nothing' philosophy, is very much in the tradition of the cottage garden.

Roses

Unkempt about those hedges blows
An English unofficial rose.

RUPERT BROOKE'S LINES describe perfectly the casual charm of cottage garden roses, their soft, simple flowers borne airily on gracefully arching stems. Little wonder that for centuries the rose has inspired generations of painters and poets, earned the devotion of gardeners in town and country and has become not only a national symbol, but the very epitomy of an English flower.

As cottage garden plants, roses are so traditional, so well loved that they deserve a great deal of our attention. Happily, attention in practical terms is only modestly demanded by the old-fashioned shrub and species roses, for they are, by and large, most amenable plants, thriving in most soils except those that are cold and wet or desperately lacking in organic material. Preferring to bask in full sun, they will nevertheless tolerate dappled shade.

As for care, they respond well to nourishment each year in the form of good old-fashioned well-rotted farmyard manure or, in its absence, well made garden composts or an organic feed like bonemeal. The shrub roses do not need pruning so much as thinning out in winter or early spring; simply cut out useless old, worn-out branches and thin any growth that is causing overcrowding and preventing the circulation of light and air, or that may spoil the shape of the plant.

In return for such modest attention, cottage roses delight both sight and smell with an abundance of richly-scented blooms in shades from pure white and the delicate hint of pastels to rich, brilliant hues of crimson and purple. The large, brightly coloured hips continue to stipple the garden red and orange long after the autumn leaves are fallen and crushed underfoot.

With such a wealth of natural beauty from which to choose, it was far from easy reaching decisions on the roses that we would show in our cottage garden and recommend others to grow. We reckoned that most people who love the old-fashioned roses would, like us, want to grow some for the purely sentimental value of their long-lived tradition and popularity and others because they are also beautiful, valuable garden plants in their own right.

The delicacy of shape and colour of the 'wild' roses of the hedgerow is perfect for cottage gardens

CRAB
APPLE.
PYRUS
MALUS.
DOWNY-
LEAVED
ROSE.
ROSA
TOMENTOSA.
COMMON
DOG
ROSE.
ROSA
CANINA.
BLACKTHORN or
SLOE.
PRUNUS
SPINOSA.

In addition, we must consider that some newer shrub roses are no less delightful in appearance, but perhaps more practical for very small gardens, being less vigorously rampant in their growth and — an advantage in any garden — blooming through many months of the summer rather than just once a year and no more.

We have settled eventually on an attempt to identify the best — or rather, a selection of the best — of both worlds, combining the old-fashioned roses with others that may be more recent introductions but are, nevertheless, in keeping with the style that we seek to achieve.

It should be said straight away that this selection of newer varieties consists entirely of shrub roses, which are excellent plants and really too little grown; too little acknowledged for their beauty and value. It does not include any hybrid teas, nor any floribundas. These more sophisticated modern introductions are too far removed from the spirit and shape of the old roses, lacking their grace and fluidity; they are sometimes too formal, sometimes too pushy and blousy. Although as individual blooms and cut flowers hybrid teas and floribundas are often exquisitely beautiful, as garden plants the bushes *en masse* are rather stiff, the flowers being dotted against the foliage rather like currants in a bun. As with bulbs, the colours of these newer, hybridized flowers are often too harsh to blend harmoniously with the traditional cottage flowers and they are much more demanding plants to grow.

If the old-fashioned shrub and species roses are simpler to grow, the same cannot be said for their history and classification. To the complete novice, a glance through the appropriate section of many gardening books or even a rose grower's catalogue can be quite bewildering and even to rose experts and historians the subject is not an exact science — hardly surprising when you consider that the history of the rose is as long as the history of civilization.

In an attempt to simplify matters, we decided to recommend, as an introduction for cottage gardeners, just one or two of the best known and most beautiful or most cottagey of each of the various types of old-fashioned roses. These types include *Rosa alba*, *R. gallica*, damask roses, moss roses, cabbage roses and briars — all these flower once each summer and most are large, spreading plants.

Then there are hybrid musks, China roses, *Rosa rugosa*, bourbon roses and hybrid perpetuals — all these are repeat flowering, blooming continuously for several months and again most are large plants. Our selection from both is inevitably a personal one, but as always, we have tried to recommend the familiar and available and to avoid the obscure.

Rosa alba, the white rose, is far from obscure. It has been grown in England since the Middle Ages and most varieties have a characteristic grey-green foliage. *R. alba semi-plena* is the white rose of York; an arching bush 4–6 feet (1.2–2 m) tall with wonderfully scented milk-white, semi-double blooms. Many varieties of *R. alba* are delicately tinted pink and perhaps best of all of these is 'Great Maiden's Blush' — a wonderfully descriptive name for the rose that was most commonly found in the gardens in *Lark Rise*; because of its familiarity, Flora Thompson tells us it was considered by the cottagers to be rather plain and commonplace. The bush grows 6–8 feet (2–2.5 m) tall, with a mass of sage-green foliage and has a spread of up to 4 feet (1.2 m), so it is essential to allow plenty of space when planting.

'Frail the white rose and frail
are
Her hands that gave
Whose soul is sere and paler
Than time's wan wave.

Rosefrail and fair — yet
frailest
A wonder wild
In gentle eyes thou veilest
My blueveined child.'
'A Flower Given to My Daughter' by *James Joyce*

Rosa gallica (literally, the French rose) was native to western Asia and southern Europe and is thought to have been known to the Medes and the Persians in the twelfth century B.C. It is, moreover, probably the ancestor of our modern garden roses. *R. gallica* 'Officinalis' is a small shrub, producing semi-double blooms that are rich both in fragrance and their crimson colour. It is known both as the red rose of York and as the apothecary rose, in reference to the importance it once carried as the basis of a thriving industry in France, where the dried, powdered petals were used in preserves and confections.

R. gallica 'Versicolor' is also known as *Rosa Mundi*, probably after Rosamund Clifford, the mistress of Henry II. The flowers are semi-double and have striking colouring — deep, rich pink striped and splashed with white.

Another rose whose petals have traditionally been used in industry — in this case the perfume industry — is *Rosa damascena*, the damask rose. Its large, powerfully scented blooms are simple in appearance and vary in colour from white to red; one or more of its varieties are used in the production of Attar of Rose perfume in Bulgaria.

Again, the damask rose makes quite a large bush, but its traditions and its wonderful perfume make it well worth growing; you have only to see the exquisite, ruffled white blooms of the variety 'Mme Hardy' to understand why Oscar Wilde wrote in his poem, 'The Garden of Eros':

> Long listless summer hours when the noon
> Being enamoured of a damask rose
> Forgets to journey westward . . .

If the damask rose was inspiration to a poet, the cabbage rose, *Rosa centifolia*, was known as the 'rose des peintres' in acknowledgement of the association of the full, double blooms with the old Dutch Masters.

There are many forms of the cabbage rose, but perhaps the best known group to have arisen from it are the moss roses. These are the full blooms that one associates with a Victorian posy and are characterized by the sticky, moss-like layer of bristles that covers their branches, flower stalks and sepals, giving off a smell rather like balsam when touched. One of the most striking moss roses is 'Nuits de Young'; the bush grows 4–5 feet (1.2–1.5 m) tall and the flowers are like soft, deep purple-maroon velvet with a centre of glowing gold.

One of the roses most traditional to cottage gardens was the simple, wild, wayward sweetbriar, commonly known as eglantine and familiar as one of the flowers in Titania's bower in *A Midsummer Night's Dream*:

> I know a bank whereon the wild thyme blows,
> Where oxlips and the nodding violet grows
> Quite over-canopied with luscious woodbine,
> With sweet musk-roses, and with eglantine.

The apple scent of the leaves is most pungent after rain; the simple, pale pink petals are easily blown along the hedgerow, the rain or dew sticking them to leaves like confetti after a wedding and the flowers of June are followed in autumn by a mass of full red oval fruits. This delightful native rose makes a good hedge — if a rather vigorous one — and has given rise to very many hybrids, for those who prefer more range and sophistication in flower colour.

R. alba *'Great Maiden's Blush'*

R. gallica *'Officinalis', the red rose of York or Apothecary's rose*

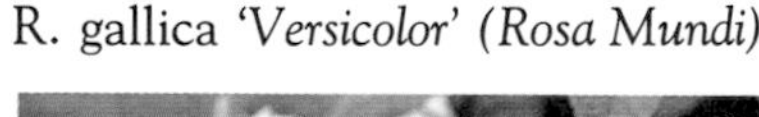

R. gallica *'Versicolor' (Rosa Mundi)*

The full, double bloom of the cabbage rose

The Scotch rose (*R. spinosissima*) is also commonly referred to as Scotch briar, although as a plant it is distinctly different in shape from sweet eglantine. It is a most useful garden shrub, consisting of a dense thicket of straight, upright branches which reach 3–4 feet (1–2 m) in height and increase in number by suckering. The slender branches are covered in prickles and bear small leaves and a mass of small flowers in white or pink, followed in autumn by shiny blackish maroon hips. 'Double

The distinctive black hips of Scotch Briar

The bourbon rose 'Commandant Beaurepaire'

R. bourboniana *'Boule de Neige'*

Musk-scented 'Penelope'

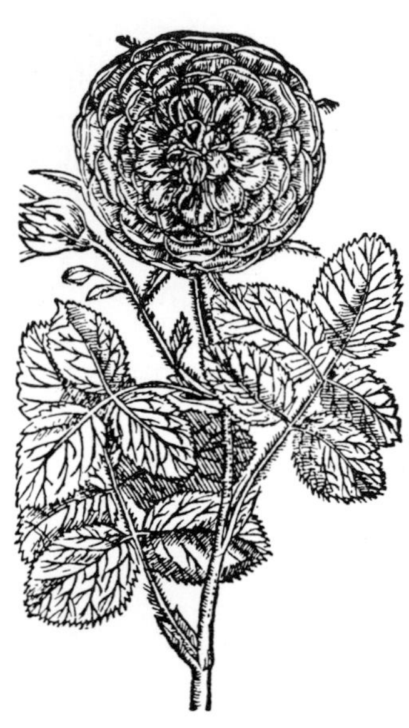

Pink' and the shaded pink 'Duke of Argyll' are particularly attractive.

These summer flowering roses are joined by several species — those wild plants found in their natural state and, although most are rather large, one in particular is worth mentioning. *Rosa moyesii* can romp away to 10 feet (3 m) tall, but the variety 'Geranium' is a more practical plant for most gardens, as it is slightly more compact in growth. However, it is, if anything, even more spectacular in appearance, with striking brick-red blooms and — especially appealing — huge, decorative, pear-shaped hips adorning the autumn branches.

One of the features that we have come to expect from roses is the pleasure that their blooms can give from June right through into the cold weather. Although all of the old-fashioned roses mentioned are beautiful plants and, size permitting, a selection of two or three should certainly feature as flowering shrubs, it is also advisable to include some repeat flowering roses to give interest for many more months of the year.

It was the China rose, *R. chinensis*, which brought to the West the much sought after trait of 'perpetual flowering' and one of the most popular and striking is 'Old Blush China' also known as the monthly rose. Its scented silvery-pink blooms are shaded with a deeper pink and they are borne in sprays on a plant 3–4 feet (1–1.2 m) tall. Not only do the flowers appear continuously, but they can be counted on to last well into a mild autumn — even until after Christmas.

From the China roses come the bourbons — handsome plants with large generous globular blooms of wonderful fragrance. Our favourite has to be 'Boule de Neige', the name of snowball very appropriate to the blooms that seem to be fashioned from scented silk of purest white and have almost the shape of a camellia. The plant, of upright habit, reaches 5–6 feet (1.5m–2 m) tall and 4 feet (1.2 m) across and is clothed in a mass of smooth, dark green leaves.

Hybrid musk roses were raised early this century, but offer a fragrance with all the heady, delicious appeal of the old-fashioned flowers. One of the best varieties is 'Penelope', which reaches 5 feet (1.5 m) high and with its strong spreading habit is excellent for a hedge. 'Penelope' is wonderfully free with her large clusters of musk-scented blooms in a pale salmon-pink, which fades almost to a creamy white.

From salmon-pink to lilac-purple, with the deeply fragrant 'Reine des Violettes' and another more deeply shaded rose of damson-purple colour, the beautiful 'Souvenir du Dr. Jamain'. Both are hybrid perpetuals, the Victorian bedding rose which, in a modern garden is more suitable for training against a wall or fence, for it reaches 5–6 feet (1.5–2 m) in height, bearing its lovely flowers throughout the summer.

If the large, vigorous, older roses would be out of proportion in your garden, or if you have space for only two or three, then you may wish to consider some of the smaller modern shrub roses that would still have the soft, airy appeal of the old cottage favourites, but on plants that are much more compact. The names of our four recommendations are distinctly feminine, giving a clue to their dainty form and gentle colours.

'Angelina' grows only to about 3 feet (1 m) in height, with a rounded, leafy shape; its flowers are quite a rich pink, opening to reveal a white shaded centre and prominent yellow stamens. 'Ballerina' is slightly taller and more open (suitable for a low hedge) and bears huge clusters of delicate pale pink, single flowers with a white centre or 'eye'.

Although her name suggests a mauve colouring, 'Lavender Lassie' is, in fact, very much on the pink side of lavender, but the ruffled, rosette-shaped blooms are fragrant and borne in large clusters on a shrub about 4 feet (1.2 m) tall. 'The Fairy', on the other hand, is a low, spreading shrub rose of the 'polyantha' type, with dense clusters of tiny, candy pink rosettes which contrast prettily with glossy, dark green foliage.

If you want something really low growing, there is a miniature ground cover rose that is truly delightful and, although modern, would blend quite happily in a small cottage garden where dainty prostrate planting that is not vigorous is needed. 'Snow Carpet' bears a mass of tiny, white cotton wool blooms on a plant with finely cut, mid-green foliage that lays flat on the ground and is, in our experience, semi-evergreen. It grows neatly to reach a spread of 2–3 feet (60–90 cm) and a group of three or five in a sunny, open place makes a most appealing feature.

From the smallest rose to the tallest — the great towering, scrambling, ramblers so familiar to cottage gardens. These are the vigorous growers that bring to life the immortal, essential concept of 'roses round the door'.

Rosa banksiae, known as the Banksian or Lady Banks rose, is very vigorous — a traditional rambler that will reach some 20 feet (4 m) in height and 8 feet (2.5 m) in spread. It is a beautiful plant to grow if you have the space on a house wall, or for an arbour or pergola, but it can be rather tender so you should grow it in a sheltered, south-facing position. The stems have very few thorns and the foliage is practically evergreen; the small, densely packed white flowers appear in May to June, creating a delightful spectacle and breathing a fragrance like sweet violets.

Also vigorous, but equally traditional is the rambler 'Alberic Barbier'. Its buds are creamy-yellow, opening to ivory-white and the flowers are generously double, contrasting with the glossy, dark green foliage.

O Rose, thou art sick!
The invisible worm
That flies in the night,
In the howling storm

Has found out they bed
Of crimson joy:
And his dark secret love
Does thy life destroy.
'The Sick Rose'
by William Blake

'Alberic Barbier', together with 'Dorothy Perkins' and 'Albertine' — two other cottage garden favourites — are Wichuriana ramblers, characterized by their vigorous growth and very long, rather lissom shoots, creating a loose, arching effect. This makes them particularly suitable for covering an arch, pergola or trellis, their lush foliage often lasting well into the winter months. In such a position the plants receive plenty of light and air, for without these essential commodities they become rather prone to mildew and damage from pests.

A better choice for growing against a wall might be one of the more modern repeat flowering climbing roses and here we are very much into the realms of personal opinion as to which varieties blend most happily with the cottage character, as well as preference of colour.

There are three that might be of particular interest; all are well established as worthy garden plants and none is too vigorous — don't expect them to reach more than 10 feet (3 m) in height. 'Aloha' has large, double, perfumed flowers of coral-pink with orangey overtones and the blooms are not dissimilar from 'Albertine', opening with a full mass of petals. One of its most useful characteristics is its suitability for a north-facing wall.

'Schoolgirl' has become a popular and well known climber — and rightly so, for against a background of large, healthy foliage of mid-green,

'Mary Rose' and 'Graham Thomas' — modern varieties bred to have the full bloom and shrubby shape of old roses, but with the advantage of repeat flowering

Albertine, a lovely old-fashioned rambler

'Dorothy Perkins' the traditional cottage rambler

'Roses round the door'

it carries soft, coppery-orange blooms that are shaded pink and beautifully fragrant. Finally, 'Zephirine Drouhin', which can hardly be described as new, since it is a bourbon climber and was introduced in 1868, but its popularity continues — often under its common name of the thornless rose, an obvious reference to stems that are almost totally lacking in thorns. The carmine-pink flowers of medium size have a rich, sweet fragrance and the plant is renowned for its continuity of bloom, although it is rather susceptible to mildew, so should be sprayed with a fungicide before the flowering season and, if necessary, further sprays applied at occasional intervals. (For those who prefer organic fungicides, they are now available, alongside stronger garden chemicals.)

Climbing and rambling roses lend themselves to just as many uses and positions in the garden as the other cottage climbers and the shrub roses can likewise be regarded as part of the overall pattern of shrub planting. Use them as occasional features amongst the traditional, mixed cottage plants — in a corner or against a wall perhaps — but do remember to allow space for the lovely arching, tumbling habit of their branches and abundance of bloom; bloom that can fill the whole garden with sweetly pungent perfume.

We sometimes feel that growing the old roses is rather like owning an antique. People in many countries have loved roses for hundreds and hundreds of years. By growing them in a modern cottage garden, it is possible to sense that you are enjoying a beauty that so many previous generations have enjoyed before, allowing the flowers a place in your life, just as they had a place in theirs.

Climbing plants

FORTUNATELY for the would-be cottage gardener, there are several really good climbers that are either essential, authentic plants for this style of garden or would certainly not look amiss. Why fortunately? Because climbers are extremely useful and advantageous in any garden, especially if you are starting from scratch on a new plot.

Have you ever watched a wall or fence become transformed in the course of one summer by a honeysuckle, or the rampant twining tendrils of a Russian vine? If so, you will hardly need telling that, when happily settled in the right conditions, a vigorous climber is capable, not just of pleasantly softening a wall, but of causing it to disappear altogether!

You may not want action of quite such dramatic nature, but in creating a cottage garden, you are bound to have need of climbers in all their cheerful waywardness and endless versatility. Perhaps it is unfair to label all climbers as wayward; some are rather neat and precise in the manner in which they travel. Maybe wilful is a better word, for in our experience, nearly every climbing plant has a strong instinct to go its own way — sometimes regardless of your attempts to bring it into line.

You plant an ivy to grow up a wall and instead it scurries back down to earth, running its tentacles in all directions along the ground. Your neighbour lovingly plants a honeysuckle and attempts to grow it along their side of the fence, but it promptly breaks through on to your side and blooms gloriously; you feel too guilty to enjoy the plant, for it is almost as though you had enticed it, like a curious cat.

The comparison may not be as eccentric as it sounds, for there is something about the way in which climbers grow that never allows you to forget that they are living things; they don't just sit there — they get up and go, often in no uncertain terms. In warm, humid weather or very gentle rain, you can almost see some climbers growing.

Such characteristics make climbing plants most useful in helping to create the effect of a casual profusion of established plants — the effect so essential to a cottage garden. As mentioned, another strong point in their favour is their versatility, for there is a climber for every situation.

They are perfect for growing against a wall or fence as a backdrop to other planting. They take up little ground space, but provide a living vertical canvas on which you can splash the impressionist shapes and colours of cottage garden flowers.

Climbers can soften a pergola, disguise a plain or unsightly shed, liven up a dead tree or stump, beautify a plain porch and even add character to the walls of the house itself. If you intend to have a cottage garden, but live in a house that could not remotely be described as a cottage, climbers could be the very thing you need to blur the distinction between house and garden; to help to unite the two and let the character of the plants themselves create a visual bond.

Most climbers are easy to grow once you have ensured that they are suitable for their chosen position. If they are to clothe a wall or fence, plant them at least 12 inches (30 cm) away from its base, but never plant against recently creosoted timber, as the leaves will burn and die.

By far the most essential climber for a cottage garden is honeysuckle — more specifically *Lonicera periclymenum* 'Belgica', a variety of the native woodbine of hedgerows and woods.

The clusters of heavily perfumed deep pink and yellow flowers curve and swirl with delicate intricacy, the stems twining, twisting and gripping firmly around their chosen means of support. On a summer afernoon, the whole plant may be humming with the activity of bees and in the evening it is the turn of the long-tongued hawk moths to pollinate the flowers.

Honeysuckle has long been a symbol of tender love and constancy and was often used to form a bower or arbour, such as the one referred to by Hero in Shakespeare's *Much ado about Nothing*:

> And bid her steal into the pleached bower,
> Where honeysuckles, ripen'd by the sun,
> Forbid the sun to enter.

It was even said that the flowers, if steeped in oil and set in the sun, 'are good to anoint the body that is benummed, and growne very cold.'

The plant is happy in most soils and likes to have its roots in cool, damp, shade. Indeed, honeysuckle does well in a particularly shady place, flowering between June and September, with red berries in the autumn. It is a vigorous climber that is most obliging in romping over a shed or dead tree, stump or some other object that you wish to disguise, although it is, of course, deciduous.

It can also be grown against a wall or fence, where it may be necessary to fix fine wires horizontally, around which the stems can twine. A mature honeysuckle grown in this way becomes rather sparse and 'leggy' at the base, a problem that is easily remedied by planting to the front of it.

Another wonderfully scented climber that has long been associated with cottage gardens is the common white summer flowering jasmine, *Jasminum officinale*. The clusters of tiny star-shaped white flowers bloom between June and September and the stems are rather fine and angular. However, foliage growth is profuse and the plant itself is really vigorous; like honeysuckle, its stems twist as they climb and therefore need some support on a bare wall or fence.

A mature climbing plant on the far wall of this cottage helps it merge with its garden and the surrounding countryside

Honeysuckle — the essential cottage garden climber, traditionally known as woodbine

The striking 'Trumpet Honeysuckle' (Lonicera sempervirens)

A well-established Parthenocissus

Clematis montana — *delicate in appearance but vigorous in habit*

Clematis x jackmanii

Summer flowering jasmine is often especially recommended for growing up into a large tree, clothing its trunk in a most attractive manner. When grown in this way, it has been known to reach 25 or 30 feet (8–10 m) in height, so its potential should not be underrated although, if it is to achieve that potential, it is as well to remember to plant *Jasminum officinale* in a sheltered spot if your garden is in a cold area.

The winter flowering *Jasminum nudiflorum* is, strictly speaking, a wall shrub rather than a climber, for it has no means of attaching itself to the wall, but is so strong in the angular growth of its branches that they support themselves in an upright position. The bright yellow flowers are one of the treasures of the winter months, appearing — before the foliage — from November to February.

Clematis is a popular flowering climber among many gardeners, but many modern, large-flowered plants in a multitude of shades, are not really appropriate for the character of a cottage garden. However, you could happily grow the original hybrid from which the showy clones have arisen — *Clematis x jackmanni* — which was raised in 1860. This is a rather spectacular climber, for not only is it quite rampant, reaching 10 or 12 feet (3–4 m) high, but from June to October it is covered in the massive, flat, rich purple blooms, measuring 4 or 5 inches (10–13 cm) across.

A less showy plant is the pretty little *Clematis montana* — at least the rather waxy looking white flowers that appear in May are pretty and tiny. The plant itself is far from small, being a vigorous and even rampant climber that loves to romp over the roof of a garage or shed and can also be used to create an arbour. For this reason, it is extremely useful — and even more so for its tolerance of a north-facing situation.

Worthy of a mention because it is, if anything, even more charming, is *Clematis montana rubens*, which has bronzy-purple shoots and leaves, and blooms that resemble nothing so much as pale pink iced flowers decorating a cake.

Everlasting pea

Another climber that can be described as charming and is certainly truly old-fashioned is not a shrub, but a perennial — *Lathyrus latifolius*, the everlasting pea. This is a traditional plant that every cottage gardener should try to grow. These days plants are only available from two or three small nurseries, for the everlasting pea is considered a poor relation to its popular cousins, the sweet peas.

However, you should not have too much trouble obtaining seeds, which should be sown individually in 3 inch (7 cm) pots in March–April. When the roots are well established, plant them in their final position in the garden. Given some support (for they grow in the same way as sweet peas), the plants will push strongly upward and in July and August will be smothered in reddish-purple flowers. As you would expect from a plant that is considered by some to be virtually a weed, the perennial pea is easy to grow and hard to upset.

Another plant that has been somewhat maligned is ivy, which is a great favourite of ours and invaluable as an evergreen climber for a cottage garden. Ivy is so useful, for it will grow in almost any soil and tolerates

dense shade; its aerial roots make it self-clinging, so it needs no help at all to climb trees, fences and walls. Not only that, its great potential as a ground cover plant should never be forgotten.

If you are planning a cottage garden without a lawn, you are bound to find yourself with bare, 'dead' areas of soil — especially in deep shade — and this is where ivy can really come into its own, as a lovely dense mat of ground cover that can easily be trimmed if it should need to be controlled.

Traditional for a cottage garden is the common ivy, *Hedera helix*, one of its most interesting and attractive characteristics being the differently shaped leaves of the climbing and flowering shoots, borne on the same plant. Other good choices would be *H. helix* 'Buttercup' with rich yellow leaves, *H. helix* 'Hibernica', the Irish ivy with dark green leaves and *H. helix* 'Tricolor', whose greyish-green leaves are margined white and edged red in winter.

If ivy is useful for winter colour, the dramatic shades of autumn are best provided by *Parthenocissus quinquefolia*, the Virginia creeper, a self-clinging vine that is ideal to clothe the high walls of a house or outbuilding. The plant is easy to grow, and pays dividends in autumn when the leaves turn wonderful shades of vivid orange and scarlet. Even in winter, the fine tracery of stems and roots is not without interest.

Vitis is a large group of climbers, commonly called simply 'vines' of various sorts, (both ornamental and bearing edible grapes) and perhaps the most useful for a cottage garden is *Vitis coignetiae*, a strong character capable of reaching the top of a tall tree. The leaves are large and attractive and, like Virginia creeper, give a superb autumn display, turning rich red and crimson.

Climbing and rambling roses complete the picture of cottage garden climbers, and they are considered separately in the chapter devoted to roses of all kinds. However, before we move on from the climbers, it is worth mentioning that, whilst it is sensible to remember when planting just how far a plant is likely to travel and how bulky it may become, it is also unwise to be too inhibited in your use of climbers, for all those mentioned can be grown in close association with other plants. Plant not just one, but two different climbers to clothe the trunk of a tree; use them to create a screen or to intermingle with other shrubs and plants. It is just this intermingling that will help to give the cheerfully rambling, yet pretty look that you seek to achieve.

Bold perennial plants

HARDY PERENNIAL PLANTS include those flowers that are most symbolic of an English summer — especially summer in a cottage garden: such flowers as columbine, delphiniums, poppies, peonies, lupins, phlox, violets, pinks and lily of the valley, to name but a very few. The climate of the British Isles seems to make it a uniquely favourable home for the plants that are hardy, but not woody like shrubs or trees, and that bear splendid flowers not just for one year, like annuals, but every year, re-appearing with a touching, optimistic dependability after the dismal wet and cold of the winter months.

Since they are permanent plants, it is essential to give perennials a good start by preparing the soil in the way already described; the initial investment in materials and effort is well worthwhile, for once the plants become established the cottage perennials need little in the way of care and attention.

Perennials can be planted at any time between autumn and early spring, except when the ground is water-logged or frozen, but the best times are late October–November or March–early April. You should obviously dig a hole of suitably generous size to accommodate the roots of the plant and it is a good idea to water the plant hole before positioning the plant and filling the soil around the roots, firming as you go.

The importance of removing the tough perennial weeds when preparing for any planting has been mentioned before, but as perennials grow during the spring months, it is helpful to run a hoe through the soil around the young plants occasionally, to loosen up the surface and remove any annual weeds that may have appeared. When the flower heads die, you may also want to cut down the stems, although the foliage should be left well alone until the end of the season. When they have died back, as part of the plant's natural cycle, the stems and foliage can be trimmed, in order to tidy up the plant and give it a clean start for next spring. If the flower heads are also left on the plants until autumn they will, of course, go to seed and you may find that seedlings appear elsewhere in the garden. We think this is rather a nice bonus, very much in the cottage tradition; if the seedlings are in an inconvenient place, they can always be transplanted once they are sturdy young plants.

A good mixture of bold perennials dominated by the tall, yellow spikes of verbascum

Although perennials may not be visible all through the year, as shrubs are, you should remember that they are nevertheless plants which will remain permanently in the garden, and plan accordingly. Plan so that there is sufficient space for them to spread themselves comfortably, displaying their full glory, but plan at the same time to mix them with shrubs, bulbs and annuals that are at their best at a different time of year, in the cottage tradition of a happy mixture offering interest at all times.

If you have a hedge or large shrubs at the back of a bed or border, leave a space of a couple of feet (60 cm) before planting perennials; this will ensure that they are not forced into leggy specimens through lack of light and air and are not starved of nourishment from the soil.

There are so many cottage perennials that it is difficult to know how to start to describe them, so broadly speaking, this chapter deals only with the larger plants — those that are good as focal points or to the rear or centre of a bed. Of course, you may not have space to grow all of them — you may not even like all of them — so it may help to separate the bolder perennials into those that are especially familiar and traditional — those which no self-respecting cottage garden would be without — and those that are less essential (although, as always, this is inevitably a matter of personal ideas and selection and even among the 'less familiars' there are some wonderful plants that are well worth getting to know).

Phlox

The first group includes the following: *Aquilegia* (columbine), *Aster amellus* (starwort), *Aster novi-belgii* (Michaelmas daisy), *Pyrethrum roseum*, delphinium, *Geranium pratense* (cranesbill), iris, *Kniphofia* (red hot poker), lupins, *Paeonia* (paeonies), *Papaver* (poppy), phlox, *Lychnis coronaria* (rose campion), *Monarda* (bergamot), *Verbascum* (mullein) and *Gypsophila* (baby's breath).

One of the tallest characters and a plant that became a real star in our own cottage garden, is verbascum, the mullein of the hedgerows. It is not dissimilar to foxglove in shape, with a mass of large, flat, grey downy leaves at the base (useful for covering the soil and avoiding a 'leggy' look) and a tall spike of yellow flowers. Probably the best variety is 'Gainsborough', which has flowers of clear, soft primrose yellow.

Delphiniums are unmistakable among the taller cottage perennials; although one sometimes sees show plants grown to fantastic size, a rather less ostentatious delphinium is not only more in keeping with the cottage look, but is also more practical to grow, as it is firmer and less likely to need staking for support — a tiresome job, especially if the flower spikes are not easily accessible. With this in mind, the Belladonna varieties such as 'Lamartine', 'Blue Bees' and 'Lodden Blue', are greatly to be recommended, for they reach only $3\frac{1}{2}$–$4\frac{1}{2}$ feet (105–135 cm) in height. Planting is best done in spring in a rich, well drained soil and it is a wise precaution to put down slug pellets in spring and summer.

Although they are available these days in pink, purple and white, the selection of cottage delphiniums really should be restricted to blue. This is far from limiting, for there is a wonderful range of blues that blend and tone together.

Aquilegia would be appealing just for its traditional common names of columbine — because the flower suggests a group of doves — or 'Granny's bonnets' which is self-explanatory. However, there is hardly a need to look to the names for interest and beauty because these qualities are well provided by the intricate delicacy of the flowers themselves.

Aquilegia is easy to grow, flourishing in sun or partial shade; the plants do not always have a very long life, but they are easy to raise from seed, and in May and June produce those exquisite blooms on rather fragile, slender stems. 'Mrs Scott-Elliott's' strain is a hybrid that bears long-spurred flowers on stems about 3 feet (1 m) tall in the typical manner of columbine. However, A. 'Biedermeier' is quite different in character and it, too, proved to be extremely popular in our cottage garden. The plant has lower, denser foliage above which appears a massed 'posy' of tiny blooms, single or double, in a rich range of colours reaching just 18 inches (45 cm) in height. This is the sort of plant that you either love or intensely dislike on sight, but it can certainly make a conversation piece in the garden and, with its massed base of fine foliage, is marvellous for filling spaces.

The twilight turns from amethyst
To deep and deeper blue . . .
. . . The twilight turns to darker blue
With lights of amethyst
from 'Chamber Music'
by James Joyce

Another superb plant for any garden, but especially one in a cottage style, is the peony, with its showy, globular blooms in pure white, soft pink or rich, ruby red; the double flowers with their generous, ruffled mass of petals are reminiscent of old garden roses and just as charming. The best

Columbines

time to plant peonies is in early autumn, and they should not be planted too deeply — ideally the buds from which growth will emerge, which are pinkish in appearance, should be only an inch or so below the soil.

Choose the situation for your peonies carefully. They prefer an open position in rich, deep soil and, once settled, resent being moved. They have been grown in gardens for centuries and many tales have arisen warning of disaster befalling anyone who tries to move a plant. Such tales probably have their origins in the commonsense fact that the plants react badly to being disturbed, but some are highly fanciful. Gerard tells us it was said that if you removed the root of a peony and were seen by a woodpecker, you were in danger of losing your eyes. The suggested solution was to tie one end of a piece of string to the plant at night, under cover of darkness, and to the other end tie a hungry dog, then tempt it with meat to pull away from the plant, thus tugging the peony out of the ground!

Lupins are one of the easiest cottage plants to grow, seeding themselves freely and developing quickly into good bushy plants. So devastating was their spreading abundance once regarded that the very name is taken from *lupus*, meaning a wolf or destroyer. *Lupinus* 'Russell Hybrids' are now most commonly available, both as seed or plants, and in a wide range of colours, although the brighter shades are better rejected.

Far from being threatening, the flower spikes of lupins are rather full, soft and gentle in appearance, both in colour and shape — in distinct contrast to the sharp, fiery spikes of *Kniphofia*, the red hot pokers, which make a dramatic focal point when the spikes — about 3 feet (1 m) tall — appear between July and September. The most cottagey variety is *K. uvaria*, which has spikey pokers of red, orange or yellow — the colours of a warm fire or a magnificent sunset on a late summer evening in the country.

Oriental poppies echo this cheerful summer red, but in the early months of May, June and July. *Papaver orientalis* is a big, spreading plant and bears huge blooms with brilliantly coloured, yet paper-fragile petals encircling an eye of velvety black. The plants may look lush, but their preference is for a poor, dryish soil; the foliage can be cut back after summer flowering to promote fresh, bolder leaf growth for the remainder of the summer.

One of the most appealing aspects of poppies is the simplicity of their flowers, and the same is true of all types of daisies, their old-fashioned charm summed up in a sentimental little rhyme by the Victorian poet Mary Howitt:

> Buttercups and daisies,
> Oh, the pretty flowers;
> Coming ere the Springtime,
> To tell of sunny hours.

In cottage gardens three types of perennial daisy were grown, all of which make good sized plants. *Pyrethrum roseum* used to be seen frequently as a cut flower; the single, typically daisy-shaped blooms with pink or white petals and rich yellow centres are borne on bushy plants with finely cut foliage, which grow to $2\frac{1}{2}$–3 feet (75–90 cm). They like a sunny position and very well-drained soil, but are easy to grow and to divide, either in early spring or after the flowers have died in July.

Aster amellus was traditionally known as starwort, in reference to the mass of small, star-shaped flowers which appear from August to October, bringing valuable colour to the autumn months. Two of the best varieties are easily remembered for their Royal connotations: 'King George' is very traditional, having been introduced in 1914, and is bluish-lavender in

Mixed deep and pale blue delphiniums

The double-flowering Aquilegia *'Biedermeier'*

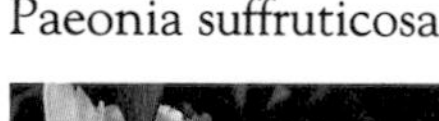

Paeonia suffruticosa

Kniphofia — the red hot poker

Informal planting which captures the mood of the cottage garden even though it includes scarlet gladioli which are perhaps a little too bold in shape and colour for the purist

Red Astilbe *'Fanal' and mauve* Iris germanica *with trollius (globe flower) in the foreground*

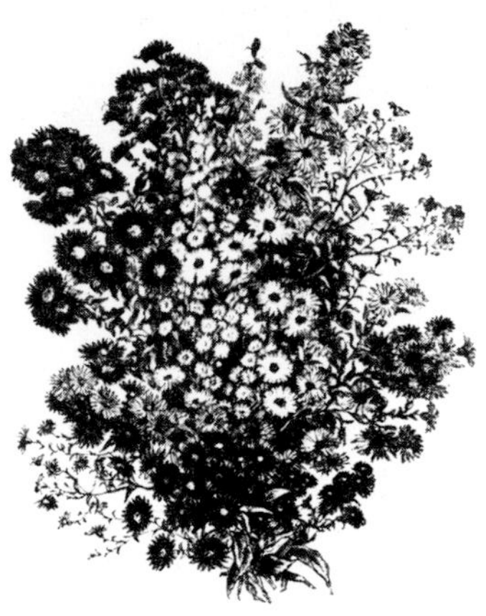

colour, and 'Violet Queen' is a lovely rich shade of violet and very free flowering.

One of the most popular old-fashioned flowers of the autumn is the best known member of the aster family — the Michaelmas daisy. Its botanical name, *Aster novi-belgii*, derives from its place of origin. Having been found by a Belgian botanist near the Dutch settlements in North America, it was named after the town of New Amsterdam which was later to become New York. How incongruous that a simple flower of the gentle English countryside should be named after possibly the world's most sophisticated metropolis!

The time of harvest celebrations and thanksgiving would certainly not be the same without the tall, leafy stems and blue, mauve and pink flowers of Michaelmas daisies, but when you buy plants, be sure that they are healthy and from a reputable grower because they can suffer from two troublesome diseases. The most drastic is wilt — drastic because there is no cure, and the plants must be lifted and burned. Mildew is the other problem, but can be prevented by planting a resistant variety such as the semi-double pink 'Tapestry' or by spraying with a fungicide before the flowers appear.

For new gardeners, *Geranium pratense* is likely to cause confusion rather than concern over disease, for this wonderful perennial plant, the common meadow cranesbill, bears little relation to the showy, colourful annual or indoor pelargoniums that we know as geraniums. Its appearance is much softer and more casual — a loose, slightly tangled mass of deeply cut foliage about 2 feet (60 cm) tall, bearing delicate blue summer flowers.

This is a must for cottage gardens, and the most available variety is 'Mrs Kendall Clarke'. She has single flowers of clear blue and is happily adaptable to most soils and situations. A great space filler that will bloom from July through to September.

Lychnis coronaria and gypsophila are two very cottagey perennials that share with cranesbill not only a delightfully soft, casual appearance with a mass of simple flowers, but also appealing, evocative common names, for the first is known as rose campion — recognizable by its silvery foliage and branching sprays of pink or red flowers — and the second as baby's breath, its myriad minute flowers creating a haze of soft, greenish white 2–3 feet (60–90 cm) high.

Lychnis was once known as *Agrostemma*, and even these two proper names have interesting derivations. Lychnis means a torch or similar light, in reference both to the fact that the leaves are soft and were thought suitable for making the wicks of candles and that the flowers are clear, bright and light-giving. Agrostemma also refers to the beauty of the flowers, for it means a crown or wreath of the fields.

In complete contrast to this simple flower of the fields are the large, showy, aristocratic blooms of the flag iris, the 'fleur-de-lys'. This is *Iris germanica*, the June flowering hardy perennial which grows from a rhizome type of root, and should not be confused with the spring bulbs of iris, which are really not authentic cottage plants.

The blooms of *Iris germanica* (also known as bearded iris) have all the exquisite grace of a ballerina, the curved, upright, 'standard' petals like raised, curving arms and the drooping 'falls' like a full, swirling skirt. The range of colours of the modern hybrids is intriguing — just about every possible combination or variation of blues, purples, white, yellow and brown. Perhaps most traditional are the blues and purples, and especially

COMMON RED POPPY,
PAPAVER RHŒAS.
GREATER CELANDINE,
CHELIDONIUM MAJUS.
YELLOW HORNED POPPY,
GLAUCIUM FLAVUM.
COMMON WELSH POPPY,
MECONOPSIS CAMBRICA.
Parts of the Common Red Poppy.
sepals
petal
stamens
pistil
fruit

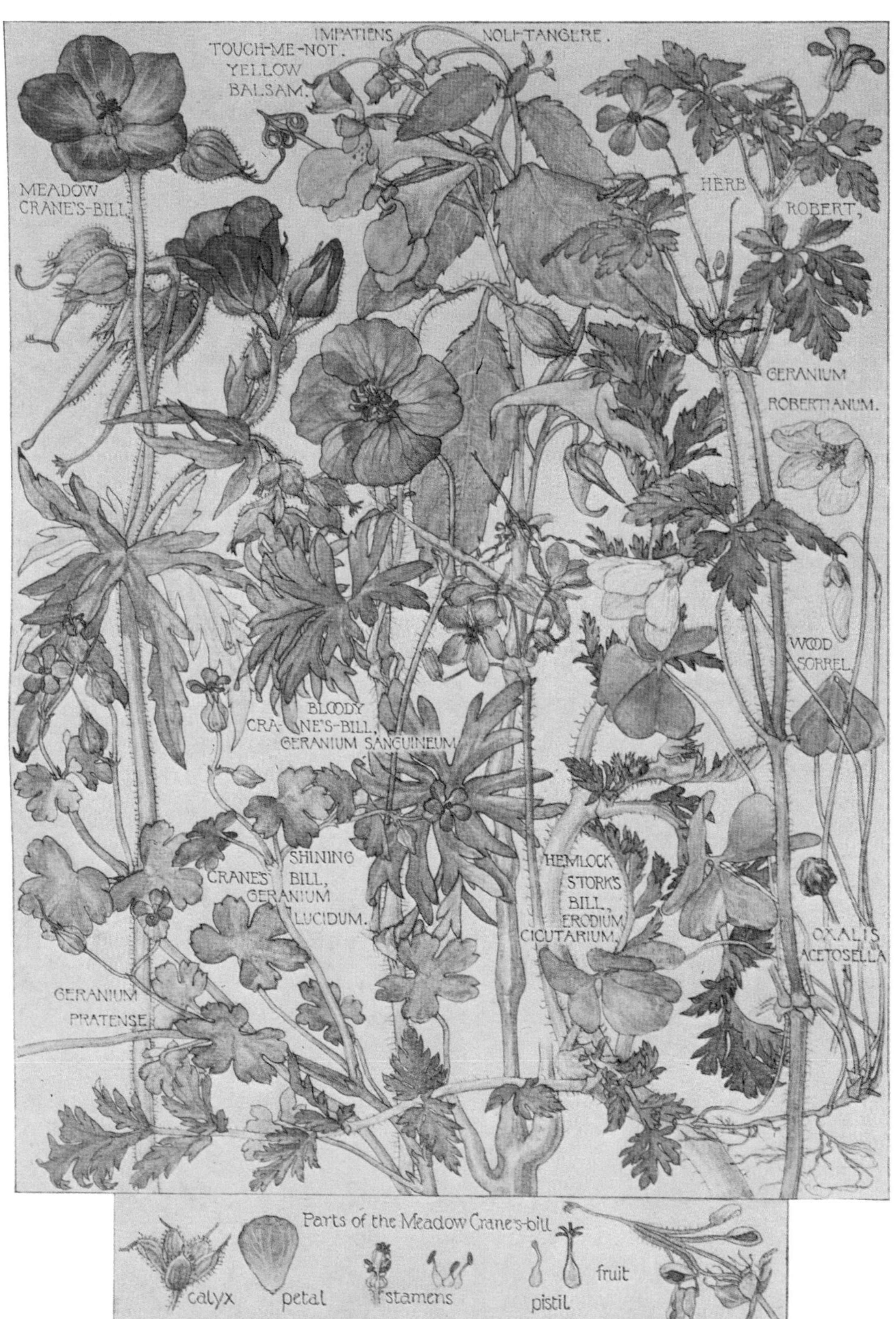
IMPATIENS NOLI-TANGERE.
TOUCH-ME-NOT.
YELLOW BALSAM.
MEADOW CRANE'S-BILL
HERB ROBERT,
GERANIUM ROBERTIANUM.
WOOD SORREL.
BLOODY CRANE'S-BILL, GERANIUM SANGUINEUM
SHINING CRANE'S BILL, GERANIUM LUCIDUM.
HEMLOCK STORK'S BILL, ERODIUM CICUTARIUM.
OXALIS ACETOSELLA
GERANIUM PRATENSE
Parts of the Meadow Crane's-bill
calyx
petal
stamens
pistil
fruit

beautiful are 'Gudrun' and 'Blue Shimmer'. If you are making a cottage garden in town, then flag irises would be useful and important plants, for they thrive on poor soil that is well drained and are reliably resistant to pollution. Plant the rhizomes in a sunny spot between July and September, setting them barely below the surface of the soil, but ensuring that the fibrous roots are spread out and buried deep.

Although other medium sized or tall perennials may have names that are less familiar to new gardeners than poppy, lupin or iris, they include some cottage plants of real old-fashioned charm like astilbe, bleeding heart or Solomon's seal, plants that are understated yet have a simple loveliness.

Polygonatum multiflorum or Solomon's seal is an interesting plant. You see its individual, arching, leafy stems lurking in damp, shady corners where, left to its own devices, the plant spreads well and in early summer each stem is laden with light clusters of long, narrow, white pendulous flowers, hanging clear of the almost upturned leaves. However, its interest lies not only in its appearance but also in its uses in medicine, for Gerard explains that its root, pounded whilst fresh and green, was considered most efficacious for healing bruises, including those occasioned by falls or 'womens wilfulness, in stumbling upon their hasty husbands fists, or such like.' He also, rather more seriously, explains that it had previously been considered dangerous if taken internally, but reports amazing results in people of all ages and even cattle suffering from broken bones, if the pounded root was given in ale to drink. This important ability to seal bones was one theory for the origin of the plant's name.

For the source of bleeding heart, the common name for *Dicentra spectabilis*, we need look no further than the shape of the dainty flowers, which hang like charmed pink and white lockets from the plant's arching stems. Dicentra makes a plant about 2 feet (60 cm) tall and slightly spreading in shape, the flowers appearing in May and lasting for several weeks; it is quite undemanding, benefiting from shelter from strong winds and a reasonable soil that is well drained.

But had I wist, before I kist,
That love had been sae ill to win,
I had lock'd my heart in a case o' gowd,
And pinn'd it wi' a siller pin.
from An old Scottish ballad

Astilbe is a little more particular; like Solomon's seal it thrives in damp, shady places, moisture being particularly important. To ensure that the soil retains sufficient moisture, plenty of peat and compost should be added when planting, and a mulch of peat whilst the plants are dormant. There are a number of hybrid astilbes which, although fairly modern, are appropriate for cottage gardens because of their thick, feathery plumes, borne in a gently waving mass above a mound of finely cut foliage that is really dense, and therefore extremely useful in the garden, especially for a moist position such as the bank of a stream or beside a pond. These hybrids, which grow 2–2½ feet (60–75 cm) tall, include 'Fanal', a deep, fluffy red; the clear pink 'Hyacinth' and the lovely 'White Gloria'.

Another cottage plant that is useful for a damp, shady position is *Hemerocallis*, the day lily, so called because its gorgeous yellow or orange lily-like blooms — thrown up on long, lissom stems above the clump of arching, sword-like leaves — last but a day or two. However, the effect of these precious, short-lived trumpet shaped flowers is far from fleeting, because they go on and on appearing for several weeks of the summer, and the rush-like clumps of leaves are useful for many more weeks besides.

Like hemerocallis, hostas are wonderful plants for foliage effect in a damp, shady spot. The usefulness and beauty of their large leaves cannot be praised too highly, and it is for these that the plants are usually grown rather than for their lavender coloured flowers, which rise on slightly untidy, leggy stems, almost spoiling the fresh, dense effect given by the foliage in the early months of summer. Given reasonable moisture, hostas (commonly known as plaintain lilies) are easy and reliable plants to grow and a wide range of effects can be achieved by the variety of foliage texture and colouring. Among the most traditional is *H. albo-marginata*, which grows 1–1½ feet (30–45 cm) tall, and has green leaves with a white margin which looks as though it might have been added by a painter of unsteady hand. *H. fortunei* is also traditional, and has lush, glaucous leaves; its various forms offer white and gold variegations to give a light, verdant look.

Even these beauties do not exhaust the selection of the bolder cottage perennials from which you can choose. There are besides the sunshine yellow, single flowers of coreopsis which bloom profusely between June and September, or the equally brilliant golden, daisy-like blooms of doronicum, appearing in April, May and June on a plant that is wonderfully easy to grow just about anywhere in the garden.

If the bright shades of yellow and red appeal to you, there are four more interesting cottage characters from which to choose. *Euphorbia* or spurge is an easy, adaptable plant to grow, its useful, spiky foliage lasting right through the summer, long after the sulphur yellow flowers of April and May. However, if severed in any part, spurge gives off a milky juice that is said to be capable of causing dermatitis. Gerard had the misfortune of taking a drop of the juice in his mouth 'which nevertheless did so inflame and swell in my throte that I hardly escaped with my life.' However, he goes on to say that this juice mixed with honey is capable of removing hair, if applied in the sun. Moreover, it has long been believed effective in the treatment of warts.

Gaillardias combine reds, yellows and oranges in flowers like large-centred double daisies on stems 2–3 feet (60–90 cm) tall. They do best in a poor soil rather than a rich one, and bloom in June; in August it is helpful to cut the plants hard back, as they benefit from the encouragement of new growth for the following year. Perhaps the most striking variety is G. 'Wirrall Flame', its browny-red petals tipped with gold indeed appearing almost to flicker like flames.

Geum 'Mrs Bradshaw' has a mass of small, bright red flowers that are borne on slender stems about 2 feet (60 cm) tall between June and August. However, the plants can be short lived and the stems rather prone to floppiness, so a good alternative is the lower, more compact *Geum borisii*, its orangey-red blooms borne above clumps of dense, mounded foliage.

The massed, golden bloom of rudbeckia appears just when it is most needed in the garden — between late July and October; it is an easygoing

Dicentra spectabilis *(bleeding heart)*

The short-lived but spectacular blooms of hemerocallis (day lily)

Astilbe and polygonum — lush waterside planting

Hosta *'Aurea Marginata'*

plant that spreads well but, being rather greedy for food, will benefit from the application of soil with fertilizer around the base after two or three years.

The taller and medium-sized cottage perennials illustrate well the widely ranging character of the authentic, traditional plants. As we've said, you would be hard pressed to grow every single one in a small garden,

Coreopsis *'Sunray'*

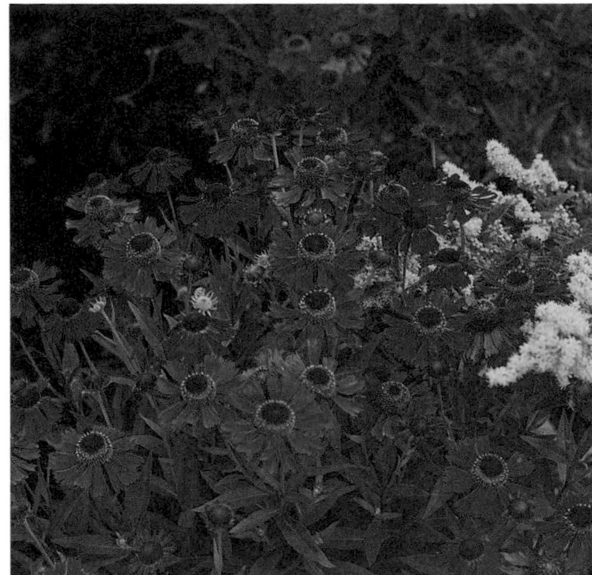

Helenium

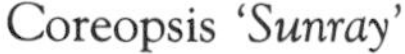

Geum *'Mrs Bradshaw'*

and a selection of the other types of cottage plants besides; moreover, it is much better to grow effective, good sized clumps of your particular favourites rather than one each of everything. So by choosing carefully you can enjoy a succession of colours, both rich and delicate, and interest, both bold and fragile, for many months of the spring and summer.

Low growing perennials

LIKE THEIR TALLER counterparts, the low-growing hardy perennials are plants that should find a permanent place in the garden, even though they are dormant during winter months. Most grow to form attractive, informal clumps or drifts, spilling over the front of a bed, softening a path or paving, forming ground cover under larger plants. Some are lovely beside water, others like to bask in warm sunshine, and among them are those flowers that are truly old-fashioned and perhaps most cottagey — such shy, sweetly perfumed delights as pinks, violets, violas, pansies, primroses and auriculas.

The botanical name for pinks is *Dianthus*, from the Greek words meaning 'divine flower', and who would argue with that? From the charmingly wayward habit of their silvery stems and foliage to the delicate tracery of their myriad scented blooms, pinks are perfection in miniature.

Perhaps it would be truer to say that the old-fashioned pinks have, almost more than any other cottage flower save the auricula, inspired gardeners to breed blooms in a continual search for greater perfection. Pinks were mentioned by Chaucer, were well loved in Elizabethan times, became one of the 'florists' flowers' bred for show in the eighteenth century and were extremely popular amongst the Victorians.

Gerard knew them as 'clove gillofloures', and later they were called simply gillyflowers, which probably means 'clove-scented' from the French *giroflier*, a clove tree. The clove-scented pinks were particularly in demand in the Middle Ages for flavouring wine and ale, which gave them the curious name of 'sops-in-wine' — a name they retained for several centuries. Moreover, Gerard tells us that a conserve made of clove-scented pinks and sugar 'is exceeding cordiall, and wonderfully above measure doth comfort the heart, being eaten now and then.'

The old-fashioned or cottage pinks were prized for their colouring and markings as well as for their scent, especially after the introduction of laced pinks — flowers whose petals are laced with the same colour as the middle zone on a background of either white or another colour; fine varieties that are still available today are 'Laced Romeo' — creamy white flowers with a reddish lacing — and 'London Delight' — mauve with a purple 'eye' and lacing. Also still available, happily, is the ultimate cottage pink, 'Mrs

Sinkins', a white, clove-scented variety that was registered in 1810, and should have a place in any modern cottage garden.

In common with all the garden pinks, 'Mrs Sinkins' is hardy (much hardier than carnations) and extremely tolerant of pollution, making them excellent plants for town as well as country. The old-fashioned pinks only flower once, and so you might consider growing also a selection of more modern, repeat-flowering varieties that are not out of keeping, such as dark crimson 'Ian', double white 'Iceberg' or sugar-pink 'Sandra', all of which are sweetly scented.

The fairest flowers o' the
season
Are our Carnations and
streak'd Gillyflowers
from 'A Winter's Tale'
by William Shakespeare

Primulas in all their variety are an essential feature of the cottage garden in spring; they thrive in rich soil in sun or partial shade and are extremely useful for moist areas beneath larger plants, in damp, boggy ground or beside a pond or stream.

The commonest and most traditional must be the primrose — a plant so familiar as a wild flower that we hardly think of it as a garden subject, but cottage gardeners certainly did, and they grew not only the common pale yellow *P. vulgaris* but also double varieties and coloured primroses — mauves and blues being most popular — and varieties with such wonderful names as 'Jack-in-the-Greens' and 'Hose-in-Hose'.

In the wild, primroses look enchanting. If you see them, please leave them for others to enjoy and do not be tempted to dig up plants for your garden; they are easy to grow from seed, which is readily available, and once established spread rapidly by self-seeding.

A much bolder traditional primula is *P. denticulata*, the drumstick primrose whose name perfectly describes the effect of its dense, globular mauve flower head as large as 2–3 inches (5–7.5 cm) in diameter and borne on stems about 1 foot (30 cm) tall. Plants are easy to grow; the leaves form large, bold clumps and, in our experience, the flowers last wonderfully well.

A primrose by a river's brim
A yellow primrose was to
him,
And it was nothing more.
William Wordsworth

The shyest and most dainty primula must be *P. veris*, the wild British cowslip, and the most brilliant, most showy are the border auriculas. Although descended from a mountain plant, the auriculas are capable of withstanding amazing amounts of dirt and pollution in the atmosphere, and became perhaps *the* favourite flower bred for show by the weavers and other afficionados of the florists' flowers. Many hundreds of varieties have been bred over the years, in all manner of brilliant combinations of blues, purples, yellows, reds and even browns and greens; some are simply hard to believe, looking just as though they had been intricately painted by hand.

Although the often equally colourful and varied polyanthus survives as a popular plant in modern gardens (and is indeed worthy of inclusion in a cottage garden) it is nice to think that contemporary cottage gardeners might make an effort to grow a selection of border auriculas, from sentiment and acknowledgement of their long history, as well as for their striking appearance.

Everything that is shy, sweet and dainty in cottage flowers seems to be embodied in our native, wild sweet violet, *Viola odorata*. This plant is a must for a cottage garden, and invaluable for establishing in an odd corner

Clumps of low and creeping perennials spill over a garden path

Violas

Parts of the Field Pansy, Viola arvensis.
MARSH VIOLET
VIOLA PALUSTRIS.
WOOD VIOLET,
VIOLA SYLVESTRIS, var. Reichenbachiana.
sepal
FIELD PANSY
petals
VIOLA ARVENSIS.
stamens & pistil
fruit shewing the seeds
DOG VIOLET,
VIOLA CANINA
SWEET VIOLET,
VIOLA ODORATA.
HAIRY VIOLET,
VIOLA HIRTA, var. calcarea
SEA PANSY,
VIOLA CURTISII.

To gild refined gold, to paint
the lily,
To throw a perfume on the
violet,
To smooth the ice, or add
another hue
Unto the rainbow, or with
taper light
To seek the beauteous eye of
heaven to garnish,
Is wasteful and ridiculous
excess.
from 'King John'
by William Shakespeare

where it can ramble and spread to its heart's content. Violets like a shady, moist position in rich soil and will reward with their lovely little flowers very early in the year — excellent to pick and have indoors as a perfumed spring posy.

If there is something touching about the delicate beauty of violets, the name and old-fashioned associations of pansies (*Viola tricolor*) is equally moving, for the word derives from the French *pensées*, meaning thoughts, in reference to the thoughts that lovers hold for each other, and the old name of heartsease symbolized the rest that eventually came to the hearts of young girls who died of love.

These days pansies are so readily available as plants in bloom that it is easy to forget their less spectacular relatives, the violas; but bedding violas come in a superb range of colours — often delightfully dusky and subtle, and their blooms will last right through the summer.

A typical cottage garden could hardly be described as being short of summer colour, but there is one particular cottage plant that was especially prized for its show of blooms during the long, dull, winter months — the Christmas rose, *Helleborus niger*. In direct contrast to its name, the plant bears pure white, single flowers as much as 3 inches (7.5 cm) wide on stems about 15 inches (38 cm) high. It thrives in moist, well drained soil and will

Christmas roses

There's rosemary, that's for
remembrance;
pray, love, remember; and
there is pansies,
that's for thoughts.
from a speech by Ophelia
in 'Hamlet'
by William Shakespeare

Double buttercup

Marsh marigold

Perennial daisies

naturalize in a partially shady position, blooming from November right through to March and making excellent cut flowers.

Helleborus is a member of the buttercup family, and therefore a relative of *Ranunculus acris* 'Flore Pleno', a rather laborious name for the simple but lovely golden yellow double buttercup, known by cottagers as yellow bachelors' buttons. The plant is not only nicely traditional, but also gratifyingly easy to grow, flourishing in ordinary garden soil and reaching 18–24 inches (45–60 cm) tall with a mass of button-like blooms.

Two further members of the family are the pretty, traditional waterside plants the marsh marigold (*Caltha palustris*) and the globe flower (*Trollius*) — both of which proved to be real eye-catchers in our own cottage garden. Like buttercups, both plants bear golden yellow blooms, the marsh marigold's being cup shaped and the globe flower's just as rounded as the name suggests. Both, too, are suitable for pond and poolside planting, for boggy areas or even a border with deep, rich, moist soil.

Two other plants that deserve consideration for damp, shady areas are *Bergenia cordifolia* with its large, circular, dark green leaves that lie close to the ground in lovely sturdy clumps and, in contrast, the host of delicate ferns that are so useful for thrusting their feathery tentacles from the base of a wall or from rocks close to a stream or pool.

The shady areas of a cottage garden would hardly be complete without that old English favourite, lily of the valley (*Convallaria majalis*). The furled, lush leaves surround slender stems from which the feather-light, pure white tiny bells dangle and dance; the flowers appear in April–May and are richly perfumed and the plants should be left undisturbed for as long as possible. Eventually they may spread to the point of overcrowding; when this happens, the crowns can be lifted and separated (best done in September–October) and the surplus crowns distributed among friends and neighbours.

In complete contrast to the seekers after cool, dank shade are the spreading sun-lovers of the cottage garden — the tiny, low-growing flowers which thrive in hot, dry conditions and lend themselves so well to softening areas of shingle or the spaces between stones.

The association with stones brings immediately to mind stonecrop (*Sedum*) which will, in fact, grow in partial shade as well as sun, but is not averse to dry conditions and will settle happily in crevices and similar nooks and crannies. The dense mat of thick, fleshy leaves which vary from shades of green to red and purple is surmounted in late summer by a host of tiny flowers on long, slender stems which create an intriguing and pleasing contrast.

The saxifrages are a similar type of plant, the most traditional being *Saxifraga umbrosa* — the familiar London pride — and another feature of many cottage gardens was *Sempervivum tectorum*, the houseleek, which was often grown on the roof of a cottage or outhouse in the belief that it would protect the building from lightning.

Tough, grassy ground cover can be provided in excellent fashion by thrift (*Armeria*). Dense cushions of spiky foliage are studded in May and

Dianthus *Allwoodii, a perpetual flowering pink that blooms from June until September*

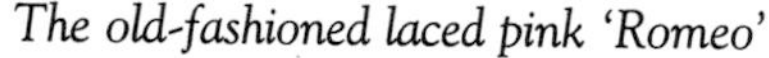

The old-fashioned laced pink 'Romeo'

Helleborus, the Lenten rose, brings welcome colour to the early spring

Caltha palustris — *marsh marigold*

June with a mass of little, rounded, pink or crimson flowers that become fluffy as they fade.

Thrift, together with *Arabis* and *Iberis*, the lovely white-flowered perennial candytuft, are much softer looking plants for dry, stony areas than two rather vivid characters that are sometimes overdone in modern suburban gardens — the bright yellow perennial alyssum known as 'Gold

Bergenia cordifolia — *an excellent plant for shade, flowering early in the year*

Campanula carpatica *forms a dense carpet of bloom, ideal between paving stones*

Sedum spectabile *'Carmen' — stonecrop*

Arabis alpina — *soft, pretty flowers for dry, stony areas*

Dust' and the familiar mauve aubrieta. Although both would have been found in cottage gardens, their more recent associations with the kind of 'rockery' that can best be described as being in the style of a dog's grave would make us feel inclined to leave well alone, and rather to make a selection from the many other pretty, old-fashioned, low-growing perennial flowers that we have described.

Bulbs

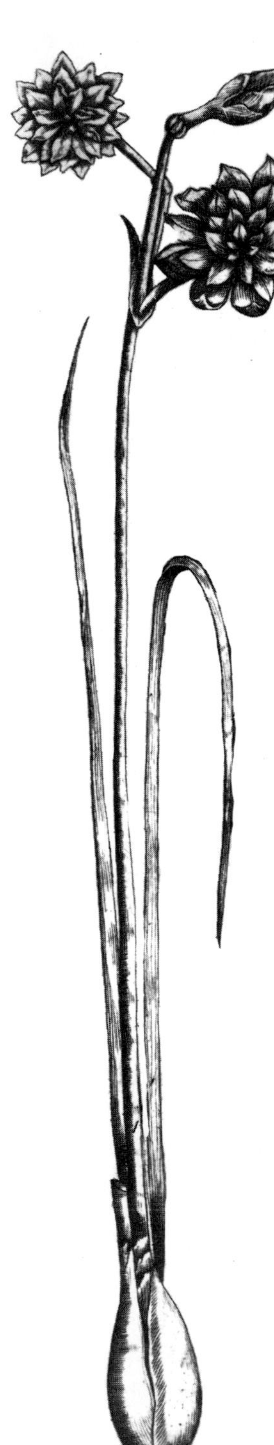

THE DIFFERENCE in style and approach between the stiff formality so beloved of the Victorian disciples of carpet bedding (and incidentally those who perpetuate the style still today) and the happy informality of the cottage garden, is nowhere more graphically illustrated than in the choice and use of bulbs.

When selecting and planting bulbs for a cottage garden, forget about the familiar dazzling colours and regimented planting patterns of bright red tulips standing to attention in rows, or huge double daffodils that seem almost to be weighed down by the might of their trumpeting, strumpeting blooms. Cottage garden bulbs are not the flashy hybridized types, but the shy, delicate, old-fashioned varieties; their flowers are often more sober in colour, but their beauty is all the more intense for the fragile delicacy of their blooms and they are deservedly loved for their reliability and ease of cultivation.

In the true, easygoing style of the cottage garden, all the cottagey bulbs can be left to naturalize in situ, lasting undisturbed for several years. This not only means that you can plan for their seasonal appearance to become a permanently recurring feature of the planting in the garden, but also that you can dispense with the annual chores of lifting, drying, cleaning, storing and re-planting.

What is more, once happily settled in their position, naturalized bulbs tend to increase rapidly, as they do in the wild, forming attractive drifts and clumps of flowers. Some spread into growing colonies at such a rate that within about five years you can lift them, divide and re-plant the bulbs, positioning the new, surplus offsets elsewhere in the garden.

Although many individual types of bulbous plants have their own requirements as to sunshine or shade, light or heavy soil, they are, by and large, easy to care for. However, it is worth remembering that all naturalized bulbs benefit from an annual application of bonemeal and those growing under trees and shrubs also welcome an annual mulch of peat or leaf mould.

When planting bulbs in a cottage garden, your guide should, in fact, be the drifts and clumps formed by bulbous plants in the wild. Try to place the bulbs so that they appear to have occurred naturally — in an uneven group rather than a neat circle or square — and remember to allow each one sufficient breathing space, for the flowers should not touch when they appear.

Again, the principle of mixed cottage planting should prevail, so that bulbs should be combined with other plants — shrubs, perennials and especially trees and even ground cover plants like ivy and periwinkle — through whose leaves they will grow, providing delicate springtime interest and colour. Plant low-growing bulbs in little clumps at the front of a border, or in drifts under a large shrub or the spreading branches of a tree. We find that drifts of bulbs are also effective in shingled areas; the shingle helps to act as a mulch and the flowers grow happily through it.

Taller flowers like lilies and crown imperials can be planted towards the middle or back of a border; again, they are most effective in uneven clumps, and are happy companions for herbaceous plants and shrubs. When they have finished flowering, their neighbours can spread to fill any gaps, especially if a strikingly attractive, later flowering plant grows to the front of the border, drawing the eye to that interest, rather than the fading bulbs. We have always been rather taken with Gertrude Jekyll's solution to the problem of disguising fading bulb foliage over a large area. She would interplant the male fern with drifts of spring bulbs, so that by early May, as the bulbs passed their best, the fresh green fronds of fern were growing up to disguise their demise and bring the promise of new growth for summer.

This may work in a small, restricted space — we have never actually tried out the idea, being aware of the fact that Miss Jekyll was describing the planting for massive borders that were planned to be the focus of attention only for the spring months. Her 'June' garden was situated elsewhere and in summer the ferns of the bulb borders were required only as a quiet background.

Nevertheless, there is one option for cottage gardeners on a smaller scale who want to avoid patches of bare soil in summer, where low-growing bulbs are at the front of a border. Experiments have shown that it is quite possible to plant narcissus and species tulips at twice the normal depth — say 8 inches (20 cm) instead of 4 inches (10 cm) and still rely upon their appearance in spring — slightly later perhaps, but with strong, thrusting growth and long lasting bloom. In summer, when the foliage has died back, you will then be able to use that soil space for colourful annuals, taking care, of course, not to disturb the bulbs when planting. If sowing seed, there should be no need to disturb the bulbs at all.

The range of bulbous plants that belong in a cottage garden is quite surprisingly wide. As well as the anticipated daffodils and jonquils, snowdrops and anemones, there is cyclamen, star of Bethlehem, crocus and winter aconite. Then there are the species tulips, their blooms sometimes reminiscent of water lilies and the real lilies, the showy aristocratic flowers — *Lilium candidum*, the divine Madonna lily, and tiger lilies with their freckled, speckled blooms. The lilies are joined by one of the loveliest and most evocative of all cottage garden plants, *Fritillaria imperialis*, the regal crown imperial.

We found that in our own cottage garden, the crown imperial took on star quality; many people who seemed unfamiliar with the plant were greatly taken by its unique shape and really rather exotic appearance. How ironic that this plant, which should seem so desirable (and justifiably so) to modern gardeners, was for many years almost despised as a rather common, second-rate flower and was kept alive in Britain largely by its survival in humble old-fashioned cottage gardens.

We know of a cottage where the elderly inhabitant has tended her garden in much the same way all her life. Villagers wait by her gate for the local bus, which comes just three or four times a day, but in April or May a long wait is compensated for by the sight of one single plant of crown imperial, blooming in all its noble glory.

The plant itself has a much, much longer history than our cottager, being familiar to cottage gardens as early as the sixteenth century and originally imported from Constantinople. The flower is indeed like a crown, with its circle of bell-shaped yellow or orange florets hanging beneath a head of narrow, upturned leaves. The phenomenon inside each bell is so delightfully described by Gerard that it would be foolish to do more than quote his words:

> In the bottom of each of these bells there is placed sixe drops of the most cleare shining sweet water, in taste like sugar resembling in shew faire orient pearles; the which drops if you take away, there do immediately appear the like; notwithstanding if they may be suffered to stand still in the floure according to his own nature, they will never fall away, no not if you strike the plant until it be broken.

It is quite a large plant, the blooms being carried on sturdy stems up to 3 feet (1 m) tall and does best in full sun or partial shade. It dislikes being moved and welcomes regular mulching with peat and one or even two top dressings of bonemeal.

Bulbs should be planted in September/October 6 inches (15 cm) deep and 8–10 inches (20–25 cm) apart and will bloom the following April–May. The flowers are orange or yellow and all varieties of *Fritillari imperialis* are appropriate for a cottage garden. The range includes orange-red 'Aurora'; brilliant yellow 'Lutea Maxima'; deep orange 'Premier' and rich, burnt-orange 'Rubra Maxima'.

Of all the plants symbolic of an English garden in spring, the daffodil must surely be the ultimate. For John Masefield in his poem 'The West Wind', they are associated with April and with a sad, tender longing:

> It's a warm wind, the west wind, full of birds' cries;
> I never hear the west wind but tears are in my eyes.
> For it comes from the west lands, the old brown hills,
> And April's in the west wind, and daffodils.

Crown imperials, although exotic in appearance, are very much in the cottage garden tradition

Wordsworth's delight in his host of golden daffodils has become sadly hackneyed and much maligned, but the poet himself noted afterwards in his diary that the best two lines in the poem 'The Daffodils' were by his wife Mary, and are at the centre of its last, reflective verse:

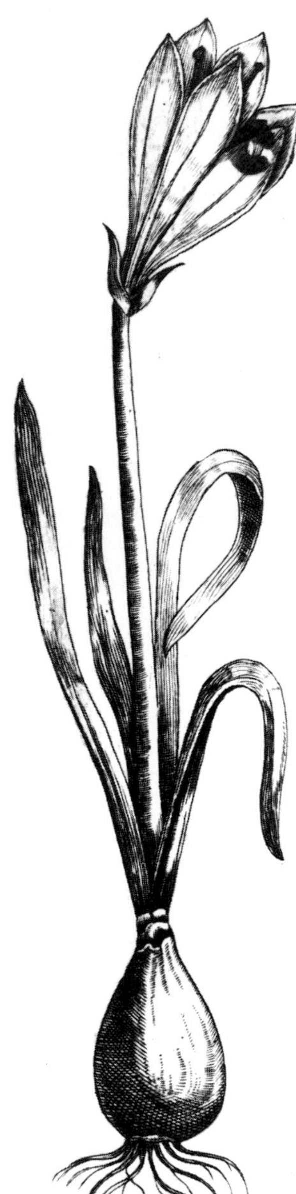

For oft, when on my couch I lie
In vacant or in pensive mood,
They flash upon that inward eye
Which is the bliss of solitude;
And then my heart with pleasure fills,
And dances with the daffodils.

Traditionally — certainly up to the sixteenth century — daffodils were considered capable of relieving not only the spirit but also the body, for the dried roots of narcissus were used to cleanse and heal severe wounds and 'stamped with honey and applied plaister-wise' they treated burns, wrenched ankles and aches and pains in the joints; applied with honey and nettle seed, narcissus root was even said to relieve sunburn.

The very name narcissus derives from the romantic tales of Greek legend, for the flower was said to spring up from the ground where the beautiful youth Narcissus fell in love with his own reflection in a pool of water. His tears of despair and disillusionment were believed to be contained in the cup or trumpet of each bloom.

However, nothing could be farther from despair and disillusionment than the jaunty appearance of daffodils growing in the wild and it is just that look which is so at home in a cottage garden. In order to achieve it, we would strongly recommend growing not the large-flowered, sophisticated daffodils, but the range of species narcissus and their hybrids which have wild daffodil characteristics; all are very hardy, standing up bravely to the elements, and are ideal for establishing permanently in gardens of any size. The range available continues to expand, with garden centres, shops and mail order firms offering greater choice each year. Many are delightful, dainty miniatures; others are as tall and stately as the bigger, bolder garden varieties and a careful selection will give a range of flowers from February right through to May.

N. lobularis (a form of *N. pseudonarcissus*) blooms in February. Its flowers have a creamy-white perianth (the correct term for the 'petals' which surround the trumpet) and golden yellow trumpet on stems just 7 inches (18 cm) tall, and the miniature golden flowers are enchanting when scattered between stepping stones and amongst shingle, increasing rapidly each season.

Equally early, but distinctly taller is *N. obvallaris*, known as the Tenby daffodil, because it has been naturalized in Wales for many years. The medium-sized, bright yellow blooms are borne on stiff stems about 12 inches (30 cm) tall.

March sees the blooming of the truly delightful rich golden yellow *N. cyclamineus*. The flowers have straight, but ruffled trumpets and the short perianth segments are backward recurved. This species is only 6 inches (15 cm) tall, but is a parent of a number of taller, truly magnificent varieties of varying characteristics.

Of these, there are four which have, in our opinion, real star quality. 'Jenny' is a pure, graceful white with a charmingly waisted cup and grows 12 inches (30 cm) tall; 'Jack Snipe' has white recurved perianths, so fine that you feel they must be fashioned from tissue paper. They make a pleasing contrast with the straight orangey-yellow trumpets and the whole nods gently on slender stems about 8 inches (20 cm) long.

N. cyclamineus 'Peeping Tom' is notable not only for its fine appearance, with deep yellow perianth and long, narrow trumpet, but also for its long lasting qualities, blooming from February or early March for at least three to four weeks.

Of all the cyclamineus hybrids it is, as so often, the baby who steals the show. 'Tête-a-tête' is one of those plants which proves irresistible at first sight, even to the hardest heart; each 6–8 inch (15–20 cm) stem produces two or three perfect tiny flowers of buttercup-yellow, the trumpet slightly fluted at the mouth and the perianth turned smoothly backward like the upturned rim of a hat. A drift along a bank, between rocks or at the front of a border can look quite spectacular.

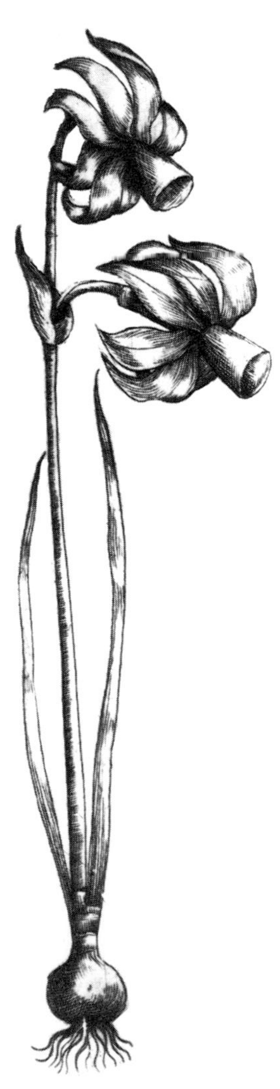

It is impossible to think of daffodils without at the same time imagining their pungent, heady scent and of all narcissus the most strongly scented is *N. jonquilla*. The jonquils have long been deservedly well-loved by cottage gardeners, who would always be attracted to a sweetly smelling flower. The blooms of the species are bright yellow, with a short cup rather than trumpet; about half a dozen are carried on each 10–12 inch (23–30 cm) stem in a cluster known as an umbel, rather resembling the spikes of an upturned umbrella.

N. jonquilla blooms in April and it is worth planting more than are really needed for garden colour, because it is hard to resist picking an ample bunch to decorate the house. (They always seem to look best just popped casually into a simple jug or pot rather than formally 'arranged'.)

All the jonquilla hybrids are fragrant and will flower from late April through into May. Two that are especially interesting are 'Baby Moon', the clusters of tiny flowers possessing a look of open sweetness and 'Suzy' which is one of those flowers so dramatic in appearance that it is hard to believe. The vivid yellow perianth is contrasted with a deep orange cup, which looks as though some gremlin has painstakingly painted each one in defiance of the usually softer colours of nature. In the garden, 'Suzy' makes a striking display, for each stem carries between two and four blooms and is 20 inches (50 cm) high.

Finally, a narcissus that will flower well into May — *N. triandrus albus*, much more attractively and evocatively known as angel's tears. In a clump amongst rocks, or to the front of the border, the shyly nodding silvery-white flowers have an understated, delicate beauty.

The narcissus may be the most familiar and popular of bulb flowers in Britain, but the tulip surely rates a close second. It seems that tulips captured the national heart almost as soon as they were introduced from their native Turkey in about 1580, for they quickly became a common sight in London gardens. Their popularity, both in country cottage gardens and in towns, is reinforced by the fact that the tulip became one of the most important of the florists' flowers grown for show and competition by people who lived and worked in cities.

The irresistible miniature narcissus 'Jumblie'

The beauty and splendour of the wild tulips — forebears of our familiar larger garden varieties — has for sometime been sadly overlooked and almost ignored by the majority of British gardeners. Yet, as with narcissus, it is the species tulips, in all their variety, that were most at home in cottage gardens, where, given a well-drained soil rich in humus and a fair ration of sun, they would naturalize and prove easy and undemanding to grow, again blending with and complementing their companion plants.

Narcissus cyclamineus *'Peeping Tom'*

The 'wild' tulips are naturally as different from each other and their horticultural descendants as chalk from cheese, but they enjoy all the attributes of modern cultivars. The bulbs themselves are rather smaller and

Wild tulip

can be planted from late September until the first hard frosts. Although they prefer plenty of sun, some responding by opening wide to reveal their full glory, they will tolerate some shade and can, therefore, be planted under a light shrub or tree as well as in more open positions.

There are now many species tulips quite readily available, from which a selection can be made. None would look really out of place in a cottage garden, but some are particularly worth noting, either for their attributes as a garden plant of all-round worth and appeal, or because they are particularly cottagey.

T. clusiana fits the bill on both counts, but especially for its association with cottage gardens. Known as the lady tulip, this is an elegant plant. The slender stems are 12–16 inches (30–40 cm) tall and the long, petal segments are sharply pointed. Inside, the flower is white with a violet centre, while the outside is cherry-red streaked with white and the very narrow leaves are often edged with red.

It is easy to see how *T. kaufmanniana* received its common name — the water lily tulip, for the deliciously coloured segments open wide and almost flatten in the sun, against a background of broad, slightly glaucous leaves. The stems are only 4–8 inches (10–20 cm) tall, further enhancing the flower's reminder of those exotic, floating lilies.

The kaufmanniana hybrids are classed as garden tulips but they, too, can be successfully naturalized; all are low-growing and bloom from March and 'Heart's Delight' is especially pretty, both in name and appearance, with its carmine pink segments edged in creamy-yellow.

Much stronger in colour and even more dainty is *T. kolpakowskiana*, which blooms in April with a golden-yellow flower, its outside splashed and shaded in coppery red tones. The leaves are narrow with wavy margins and generally lie flat, but in a sheltered, sunny spot the flowers open up like stars.

Similarly, *T. tarda* has star-shaped flowers that open wide in the sun. At first glance, you could be forgiven for wondering whether this dainty flower is a tulip at all; the white edged blooms have a wide yellow centre and grow in clusters of up to six on a stem just 6 inches (15 cm) tall. We like to grow them to complement variegated foliage, like that of a stripy grass or *Hedera helix* 'Goldheart', the green and gold ivy with neat, tiny leaves.

For those who want an excellent garden plant with stronger, brighter shades, *T. praestans* is outstanding, with its clusters of small orangey-scarlet cup-shaped flowers on 6 inch (15 cm) stems. The hybrid, *T. praestans* 'Fusilier' is, true to its name, a bright military red, yet the informality of its dark green leaves and profusion of small flowers mean that it could find a place in a modern cottage garden.

No self-respecting cottage gardener could fail to try growing lilies. Between 1824 and 1832 a Miss Mitford of Three Mile Cross wrote *Our Village*, an informative and comprehensive description of an amalgam of many Hampshire villages and gardens; in it she mentions that of the cottage bulb flowers, tulips, crocus and snowdrops were familiar and widely grown, but lilies were sought after and their possession was prized.

In fact, the supremely beautiful white Madonna lily prefers, as Vita Sackville-West once pointed out, the humble surroundings of the cottage garden to a more ambitious, gentrified setting. She goes on to wonder whether this was due perhaps to certain lowly traditions that may have been scorned by more sophisticated folk. The cottage housewife, for instance, would throw her pail of soap-suds over the flower beds. (In fact, advice was later given by more educated authorities that the young growth should be sprayed with soft-soap and water as a prevention against botrytis, a fungus disease.) Similarly, Madonna lilies like a chalk-laden, gritty soil, apparently a confirmation of the theory that they thrived in cottage gardens partly because of the grit which blew in from the lanes.

If we want to grow Madonna lilies, it is obviously expedient to concern ourselves with down-to-earth matters, but it is pleasant firstly to linger over the elegant beauty which attracts us to these wonderful white blooms, symbolic of purity and virginity — the sweetly perfumed church flower of the Annunciation and one well loved by poets.

Shakespeare called it 'A most unspotted lily' and Thomas Campion wrote delightfully complimentary lines of his loved one:

> There is a garden in her face,
> Where roses and white lilies grow;
> A heav'nly paradise is that place,
> Wherein all pleasant fruits do flow.

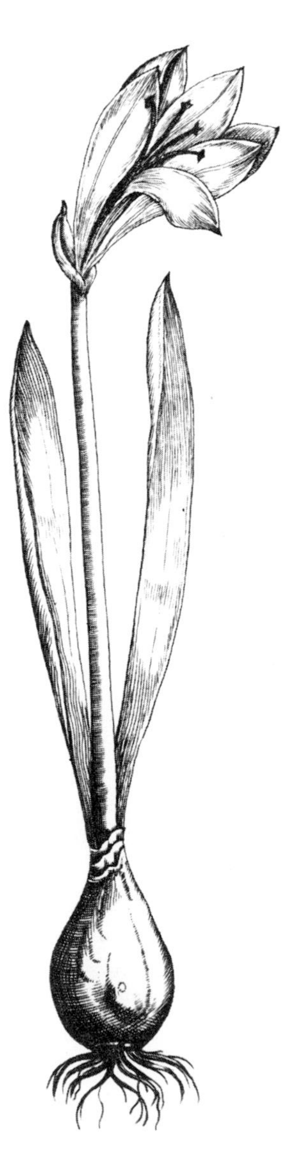

Lilies are a recurring theme in the poetry of Oscar Wilde, who wrote the beautiful line, 'White lilies, in whose cups the gold bees dream.'

Lilium candidum, the Madonna lily, is the earliest of all, bearing its chalice-like flowers on 3–4 foot (1–2 m) stems in June and July. The bulbs should ideally be planted in early September although it is safe to plant through to October.

The bulbs should only just be covered when planted — 1 inch (2.5 cm) of soil is sufficient and, as mentioned, a sharp gritty soil is best. Once planted, Madonna lilies prefer to be left alone, so don't be tempted to disturb them or move them around.

There are several important preferences that *Lilium candidum* shares with all lilium species and cultivars. Firstly, when the bulbs arrive, either plant them immediately or store them in peat and plant as soon as possible. If they are exposed to light, the scales will go soft.

Secondly, it is worth preparing the soil thoroughly before you plant, for lilies must have good drainage — even to the extent of digging out a pocket of soil, replacing the bottom layer with stones or coarse gravel for drainage and then mixing the remaining layer of soil with leaf mould or other humus material and sand. Unlike candidum, most lilies should be planted at two and a half times the depth of the bulb.

In addition to the Madonna lilies, the most traditional for a cottage garden are *Lilium martagon*, with its wonderful, prolific pink or violet coloured blooms and *Lilium tigrinum splendens*, the tiger lily, its rich orange flowers speckled black.

Tulipa turkestanica — *one of the many species tulips ideal for naturalizing*

Tulipa clusiana, *the lady tulip*

(left) Madonna lilies

At the other extreme from the tall, impressive lilies are a number of small bulbs that also deserve a place in a cottage garden and have much to contribute to its charm and interest — flowers like anemone, crocus, snowdrop, snowflake, winter aconite, grape hyacinth, *Erythronium dens-canis*, the dog tooth violet, star of Bethlehem and the diminutive cyclamen.

Anemone, like the tulip, was an important florists' flower, bred for show and competition. It was traditionally known as wind-flower, by all accounts because Pliny once observed that the flowers only open when they are blown by the wind. Certainly one of the most charming aspects of anemones is the way in which their soft, fragile petals open and close — and continue to do so for days and even weeks.

It is the hardy anemones that will naturalize and multiply in sunny or partially shady locations and in a well-drained soil that is rich in humus. The tubers or rhizomes should be planted in September or October to bloom from March to May.

The hardy souls include A. *blanda*, which has small, starry flowers of blue, white or pink and A. *nemorosa*, the wood anemone of Britain and Europe. This shy little flower will literally carpet woodland with pink and white from April into May, preferring dappled shade to any other conditions. The stems are only 1–2 inches (2.5–5 cm) tall and the leaves are covered with silky hairs.

The more showy 'poppy' anemones that one usually buys as cut flowers are not hardy and are probably less appropriate in appearance for a cottage garden, although if you don't mind taking the trouble to lift and replant each year and give the plants some care, you might grow a few for a splash of colour, or indeed for cutting.

Of the many types of crocus so familiarly and widely grown, almost any of the softer shades or dark colours could conceivably find a place in a cottage garden, but two are truly traditional — spring flowering C. *chrysanthus* and autumn flowering C. *sativus*, the saffron crocus.

C. *chrysanthus* is a hardy naturalizer that likes full sun or partial shade and sandy, peaty soil. The bulbs should be planted 2 inches (5 cm) deep, between September and November. A number of named varieties are available and they are becoming extremely popular. Some of the more unusual ones are 'Cream Beauty', which is yellow with a bronze-green base; 'Eyecatcher', in elderberry-purple, edged white and 'Gipsy Girl', a buttery-gold colour feathered with chocolate, which blooms in March.

Bulbs of *Crocus sativus* should be planted in July, immediately after purchase and in October/November, before the leaves appear, will produce the veined purple flowers of the saffron crocus, their long, red stigmata being the source of supply of one of nature's most striking products and, until the eighteenth century, the basis of a thriving industry.

Saffron was primarily produced from acres of fields of the crocus crop in the area around Saffron-Waldon on the Essex-Cambridgeshire borders and, as well as being used for the familiar yellow dye, was a flavouring for cakes and, according to Gerard, a powerful medical stimulant, for as well as simply making people lively and merry, it was used to strengthen the heart and to treat consumption and severe chest infections.

Everybody knows the common single snowdrop, *Galanthus nivalis simplex* and most people love it for its embodiment of hope and renewal as winter turns to spring. However, the double form G. *nivalis* 'Flore Pleno', is also worthy of inclusion in a cottage garden, as is the summer snowflake, *Leucojum aestivum*, which grows to 18 inches (45 cm) tall, and will flourish in damp ground beside a pool. Its nodding, pure white bells are tipped with green and measure a good inch (2.5 cm) across.

As early as snowdrops are the golden buttercup-shaped flowers of winter aconite, *Eranthis hyemalis*. On stems just 2 inches (5 cm) high, the vividly coloured blooms are surrounded by a charming green ruff, although the true foliage emerges after the flowers have formed. Eranthis naturalize very easily, spreading to form a golden carpet under trees and shrubs.

Anemones

Another rapid spreader, although rather later — flowering in May — is the star of Bethlehem, *Ornithogalum umbellatum*. As well as looking attractive, its white star-shaped flowers striped green and borne in clusters at the centre of a rosette of leaves, ornithogalum is a most obliging and useful bulb, growing almost everywhere and anywhere.

There is little more appealing than the sight of a mass of tiny cyclamen in autumn bloom in the dark, secret shade of the larger branches of an old fir tree and their romantic quality seems to have appealed equally to country people in the sixteenth century, for cyclamen, beaten and made into little flat cakes, was said to be 'a good amorous medicine to make one in love'. Its common name of sowbread has much less romantic connotations, for the tubers are favoured by swine, and in the Perigord region, pork producers claim that their product has a special flavour when the pigs are treated to cyclamen tubers.

The tubers of the autumn flowering species C. *neopolitanum* should be planted in July for July/October flowering. They are sometimes reluctant to flower in their first season, but, once established, will naturalize and spread and should be left undisturbed, for they dislike being transplanted. Some shade is essential to cyclamens and they will grow happily under conifers, so would be an ideal underplanting for yew.

With such a variety to choose from, it is easy to see that bulbous plants in a cottage garden have a great deal more to offer than the stiff 'bedding' tulips and daffodils of parks and many suburban gardens. We are certain that if you grow just some of the species and cultivars mentioned, you will be pleasantly surprised time and time again by the bright, yet fragile beauty of the flowers combined with the reliability and sturdiness of the plants.

It is also rewarding to discover that bulbs are far from being spring flowers alone; that if you start a garden early in the year, you don't have to wait until autumn to plant and the following year to see the fruits of your labours. From the earliest snowdrops and aconites to the tulips and daffodils, the crown imperials, summer lilies and finally cyclamen and autumn crocus, the cottage bulbs are truly year-round plants.

Tiny winter aconites — a splash of colour in the dark months

Star of Bethlehem

(left) An informal drift of crocus naturalized in grass

Annuals and biennials

Too quick despairer, wherefore wilt thou go?
Soon will the high Midsummer pomps come on,
Soon will the musk carnations break and swell,
Soon shall we have gold-dusted snapdragon,
Sweet-william with his homely cottage smell
And stocks in fragrant blow. . . .

Matthew Arnold

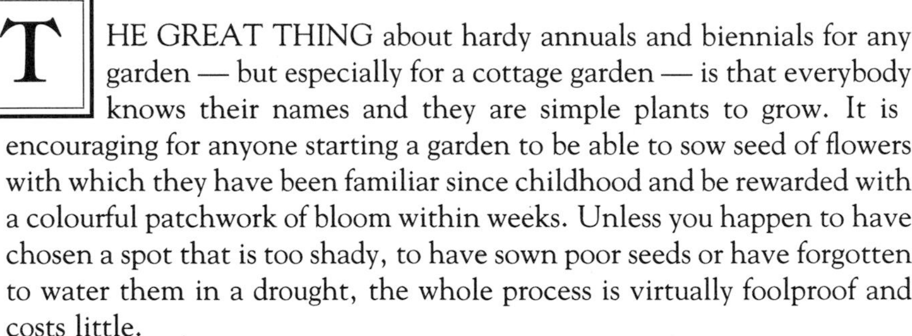

THE GREAT THING about hardy annuals and biennials for any garden — but especially for a cottage garden — is that everybody knows their names and they are simple plants to grow. It is encouraging for anyone starting a garden to be able to sow seed of flowers with which they have been familiar since childhood and be rewarded with a colourful patchwork of bloom within weeks. Unless you happen to have chosen a spot that is too shady, to have sown poor seeds or have forgotten to water them in a drought, the whole process is virtually foolproof and costs little.

Every year, it seems, the seed companies tell us that the sale of flower seeds has overtaken vegetables and that the old-fashioned flowers are becoming more and more popular. We certainly welcome that news; perhaps in a few years' time we will see more front gardens filled with the cottage flowers whose blooms dance and bob in the summer breeze, rather than stiff African marigolds and dazzling begonias!

Nearly all the cottage annuals require sun, but are unfussy about soil; they can be sown in nicely irregular patches straight into the garden where they are to grow and the seedlings thinned later; they will flower for several months until the autumn and are very handy for filling spaces in a new garden while permanent plants are becoming established. But not all annuals are authentic cottage flowers, as some gardeners have a tendency to believe, and it pays to take care not to spoil the desired effect with a gaudy intruder.

By far the largest and most exuberant cottage annual is the sunflower, (*Helianthus annus*) that golden giant whose huge, open face nods over the hedgerows in so many cottage paintings. It is a phenomenon of nature and a source of continuous amazement that such a thick, sturdy stem should grow as high as 10 feet (3 m) or more in such a short time, from one quite small seed.

The plant was introduced to Europe from Peru and Gerard refers to it as 'The Indian Sun' or the golden flower of Peru. He knew of no previous uses

Larkspur

for the sunflower, but reports that he found it extremely pleasant to eat the boiled flower buds with butter, vinegar and pepper like an artichoke!

Sunflower seeds should be sown in April and will bloom from July to September. The plants, hardly surprisingly, like a sunny situation, but prefer to have their roots in moist soil. Some people like to leave them late in the garden so that the birds can peck at their seeds.

A much more delicate flower that can also be useful for height, or indeed to create a pretty screen, is the sweet pea (*Lathyrus odoratus*). Its fragile blooms in a multitude of pastel shades and a haze of perfume are just as popular today as they were in Victorian times and new varieties continue to be introduced.

Seeds of sweet pea can be sown outdoors in March or April and need to be supported, as their tendrils reach up to 6 feet (2 m) and more — a simple trellis or the old-fashioned pea sticks would be fine. They like a sunny, open position and for a cottage garden, you should choose the fragrant varieties, preferably in mixed, soft colours. Although they are a recent introduction, the dwarf sweet peas like 'Snoopea', which grow to only 1 foot (30 cm) tall, would not look amiss in a modern cottage garden.

Larkspur is an elegant plant and very traditional, its gently waving flower spikes making an excellent annual filler where a plant about 3 feet (1 m) tall is needed in a border. *Delphinium consolida* is the tallest, softest looking larkspur, with blooms of blue, pink and white offset by fine, feathery foliage. Seeds can be sown outdoors from March to May to bloom from June to August.

If you are planning annuals to harmonize and compliment other plants, and to make the best use of their fast effect, then it is sensible to look at them in terms of their height and the amount of space they will be likely to fill (as well, of course, as their colour). In our experience, summer colour at a height of 1–2 feet (30–50 cm) comes in very handy to bridge any gaps between very low-growing plants and taller perennials like iris, peonies, *Geum*, kniphofia or poppies.

The group of cottagey annuals that fit this bill could include cornflower (*Centaurea cyanus*), love-in-a-mist (*Nigella damascena*), sweet scabious (*Scabiosa atropurpurea*), ten week stocks (*Matthiola*), tobacco plants (*Nicotiana*), snapdragon (*Antirrhinum*), mignonette (*Reseda odorata*), and toadflax (*Linaria*).

Cornflowers conjure up the warm, summer image of an azure dotted meadow in the afternoon sun. The mass of small, button flowers on long, slender stems keep blooming for several weeks between June and September and are as good to pick and enjoy indoors as to appreciate in the garden. We do feel that in a cottage garden cornflowers should be blue; although many seed packets contain mixed colours, plain blue should not be too difficult to find and is sometimes offered as part of a 'wild flower' seed range.

The name of love-in-a-mist romantically, yet perfectly, describes the flowers of nigella, forming a cloud of pale petals amongst its misty, feathery foliage. Again, to be cottagey, nigella should be blue and, as a nice

Sweet pea 'Xenia Field'

reminder of the great gardening legacy that she has passed on to us, the most popular blue variety is *Nigella damascena* 'Miss Jekyll'. 'Miss Jekyll' should be sown in early spring in a sunny place; the seedlings will need to be thinned and will reward with flowers from June to September.

Scabious creates a similar effect to nigella, although it grows rather taller, reaching 3 feet (1 m) or so. Pale blue is again most cottagey and is probably most commonly seen, especially as a cut flower — almost more than as a fragrant garden flower. It is worth growing partly because it is so good to pick and it will thrive in a sunny place, especially where lime is present in the soil.

(above) Nigella damascena, *traditionally called 'love-in-a-mist'*

(above right) Nicotiana *'Lime Green', an unusual form of tobacco plant*

(right) Tall stems of larkspur

It is a beauteous evening,
calm and free,
The holy time is quiet as a
nun,
Breathless with adoration.
Wordsworth

Nicotiana, the tobacco plant, is a most obliging and useful annual, for its leaves are bushiest at the base of the stem, covering the soil to create a matt green background against which the stems taper towards the dainty white, pale green or pink clusters of fine, trumpet-shaped flowers. It is towards dusk that the fragrance of nicotiana is at its most powerful. Evening fragrance is delightful in any garden, but is especially important in a cottage garden, where cottagers would doubtless enjoy a sense of peace after a day's work.

Antirrhinum evokes quite a different mood, with its warm yellow, orange and pink colours and its sentimental reminder of a childish fascination with the popping snapdragons or 'bunny rabbits'.

The tallest varieties of *A. majus* reach about 3 feet (1 m) tall and although they are excellent for cutting, may need staking. If your garden is in a windy spot, then grow a variety that will not reach more than 18 inches (45 cm).

Antirrhinum is really a half-hardy rather than a hardy annual, so the seeds should be sown indoors or in a greenhouse between February and April, planting out in May or June, after the danger of frost has passed. In mild areas, you could treat it as a biennial, sowing seed outdoors the previous July and transplanting seedlings in September to their final positions.

From the 'infillers' of the border, we step down to the low-growing annuals that are so attractive at the front of a bed, beside or between paving, in little clumps or as a wide, curving drift with irregular edges. If you have shingled areas running up the edge of a bed, try planting the shorter annuals both in the bed itself and spilling over into the shingle, growing through it apparently casually, but most effectively, softening and blurring edges in a manner essential to the cottage style.

Really low growers are, as mentioned, useful between paving — especially where the pieces are set apart, as stepping stones. Perhaps the best choice for this is white alyssum in a dense, carpeting mass. For a quick softening effect, two or three boxes of alyssum in flower, bought from a garden centre, would transform a stepping stone path in no time.

However, in a cottage garden try to avoid using alyssum — or any other short annual — as a long, neat line of edging, like the frill around a petticoat. This fancy effect is contrived and our aim in a cottage garden should be to echo the way in which plants grow naturally. Of course, we are not creating a 'natural' garden — perhaps cottage gardening could best be described as minimum interference with nature, rather than as natural gardening — but we think that flowered frills and formal plant patterns are rather in the category of maximum interference! So, better to plant all annuals so that they look as though they might have seeded themselves. If they merge and mix with each other at the edges, and if the odd stray crops up here and there, well so much the better.

Love-in-a-mist

In fact, the shorter cottage annuals are far from formal in character — flowers like candytuft, pot marigold, nasturtium and Virginian and ten week stocks. Candytuft (*Iberis umbellata*) has the wonderful advantages of

Pot marigold

being extremely pretty and very easy to grow, its pastel shades of lilac, pink and white being excellent for a soft drift of bloom and blending well with other pink or white flowers — especially with the similar shades of stocks.

When we included stocks in our cottage garden, several people lamented the fact that they are seldom seen in modern gardens. This is a great pity, for even the tall double ten week stocks (*Matthiola incana*, a half-hardy annual) are not difficult to grow and the little Virginian stock grows almost like a weed. Stocks come in a good range of colours from white to deep mauve and are, of course, blessed with a pungent perfume. The musty scent may be a bit over-sophisticated, although it would surely be difficult for anybody to dislike the wonderful evening fragrance of the night scented stock, *Matthiola bicornis*.

In contrast to its lovely smell, the flowers of night scented stock are rather insignificant, remaining closed during the day. For this reason, it is a good idea to plant it close to the house, where its fragrance can waft through an open window on balmy summer evenings, and to mix with it Virginian stock (*Malcolmia maritima*). The single flowers of the latter will give daytime interest and, as mentioned, it is one of the easiest of all annuals to grow; the seeds can be scattered almost anywhere and relied upon to produce flowers on 6–9 inch (15–23 cm) stems a few weeks later.

Where marigolds are concerned, it is vital to distinguish between the open, double-daisy shaped orange and yellow flowers of *Calendula officinalis* — very much a traditional cottage garden plant and commonly known as pot marigold — and the French and African marigolds (*Tagetes* of various sorts) with their heavy lollipop heads and shaded, tanny-orange blooms. These foreigners have no place in a cottage garden!

The dried petals of calendula were traditionally used in winter soups and broths, especially in Holland. The flowers are extremely easy to grow, indeed thriving best in poor soil, tolerating partial shade or sun, and blooming just a few weeks after sowing. If you pinch out the top of the seedlings, the plants will be more bushy and should carry on flowering from May or June right into the autumn.

The Elizabethans knew nasturtium as Indian Cress and appreciated the hot, cress-like flavour of its leaves in salads, and it was only a little later, as the plant became established in this country from its native West Indies, that the edible quality of the hot coloured flowers was also savoured.

As a cottage garden plant, nasturtium (*Tropaeolum majus*) is useful not only for its edible qualities, but also for its ability to wander in all directions — upwards as a climber reaching 6 or 8 feet (2–2.5 m) high, horizontally to cover bare patches or a sunny bank and even downward to trail amiably over a low wall. The adaptability of its range of varieties is helped even more by the fact that nasturtium thrives in the poorest soil, in sun or light, dappled shade and in fact may not do at all well in a rich soil.

From annuals to biennials. The seed of these should, of course, be sown in late summer, either where they are to grow or in a 'nursery bed', the seedlings then being transplanted to their flowering position in the garden during the following spring, where they will bloom in summer. The

A dramatic clump of foxgloves

The soft pink and white of ten week stocks and candytuft contrast with bright red geranium 'Paul Crampel'

Hollyhocks

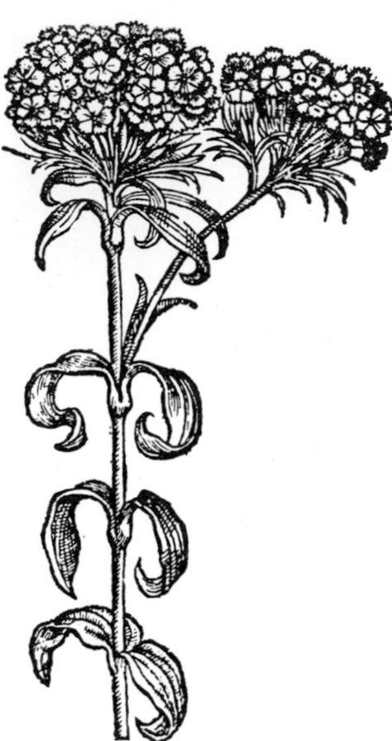

Sweet William

cottage biennials include some interesting and even essential flowers — again ranging from the gigantic to the diminutive.

Firmly in the first category are the humble hollyhocks and foxgloves — humble because they seem to spring up all over the place and it is easy to take them for granted. But take another look, as though you are seeing them for the first time; they are wonderful plants and are somehow the epitomy of an English summer — certainly the epitomy of an English cottage garden. Almost unnoticed at first, they seem suddenly to appear in all their glory — tall, stately stems covered in tight green buds that open like a slow-burning firework. There is something poignant about the fading of the last flowers of the hollyhocks, for with them summer, too, is fading as the harvest is gathered and the evenings draw in.

In the sixteenth century hollyhocks were sometimes called by the appealing name of *Rosa ultra-marina* or outlandish rose and the botanical name of *Althaea rosea* reflects that connection. Sadly, the plants are terribly susceptible to rust and for this reason are recommended to be grown as a biennial rather than the perennial that they are by nature.

Foxgloves (*Digitalis purpurea*) are even more deeply steeped in tradition — although it is a rather sinister tradition, mostly arising from the reputation of digitalis as a heart stimulant and also a fatal poison. Foxgloves are just as closely associated with cottage gardens, where they will helpfully thrive in shade, even under a tree, for they grow wild in woodland conditions.

Foxgloves will reach 4–5 feet (1.2–1.5 m) in normal conditions. For our cottage garden, we were lucky enough to have foxgloves forced to breathtaking size by one of the country's leading experts. Not surprisingly, they became quite a talking point!

There is yet another tallish character that is steeped in the tradition of cottage gardens — *Campanula medium*, the lovely Canterbury bell. In Chaucer's time the woods around the cathedral city of Canterbury were said to be full of the plants growing wild and the flowers apparently took their name from the small bells that were attached to the harness of the pilgrims' horses.

The blue and white 'cup and saucer' varieties are most traditional, the bell-shaped cup sitting on a flat, frilled saucer. The plant thrives in a slightly shady spot and will reach 2½ feet (75 cm) tall.

Sweet William (*Dianthus barbatus*) is yet another old favourite, its large flower heads making a pretty posy. Gerard referred to them as sweet William or sweet St John and tells us 'They are . . . esteemed for their beauty to deck up gardens, the bosomes of the beautifull, garlands and crownes for pleasure.'

Although strictly speaking a perennial, the plant is better grown as a biennial. If seeds are sown in June, they will be ready to bloom just one year later, and thrive in a sunny place, the bulkiness of their flowers filling a sizeable area.

A plant that one tends to associate with sweet William is the wallflower — perhaps because of its size and leafy stem and the fact that each appears at a time of year when their colour is appreciated — sweet William as one of the earliest summer flowers and wallflowers in the spring months from March to May.

It is not difficult to deduce the origin of the name of the wallflower (*Cheiranthus cheiri*), so called because it appeared so frequently springing from the cracks in old brick or stone walls. Less familiar is the use for which Gerard recommends the leaves: if they were pounded with a little bay salt and wrapped around the wrists they would, he says, 'take away the shaking fits of the Ague.'

One reason for its appearance in old walls is obviously its preference for lime in the soil and it responds to being grown in a sunny spot. By and large, it is a very easy flower to grow and you hardly need go to the bother of sowing seeds, so plentiful are the young plants available in the autumn from garden centres and shops. Shades of yellow and orange are most traditional, but crimson and even purplish-coloured wallflowers have been grown for so long that they would not look amiss in a cottage garden.

Finally, two cottage biennials of very different character, yet both with charming names and both traditional — evening primrose (*Oenothera biennis*) and the dainty little forget-me-not (*Myosotis sylvatica*). Evening primrose is quite a large plant, reaching 3 feet (1 m) in height and its stems, together with the long, narrow, crinkle-edged leaves, are covered in hairs. During the day its appearance is quite insignificant, the flowers remaining firmly closed. However, in early morning and in the evening the clusters of yellow flowers spring open to resemble large buttercups; their perfume is strong and pungent and they are frequently visited by moths and other insects of the night. This is a plant that can rapidly spread to become invasive, and one with which we are likely to become increasingly familiar as a commercial crop, for evening primrose oil is recognized as being very high in polyunsaturates.

Forget-me-not must be one of the most charming of all garden plants, with its mass of tiny, china blue flowers that appear in April–May and have long been associated with love, constancy and remembrance. Cottagers believed that if you planted forget-me-not on the grave of someone you had loved and lost, the plant would never die as long as you were still living.

From such enchanting, old-fashioned biennials we should return for a moment to a seasonal flower that is probably more popular today among all types of gardeners than it ever was among cottage gardeners — the flower that we know as geranium, although it should properly be referred to as regal or zonal pelargonium. In cottage gardens the old, orangey-red variety 'Paul Crampel' was most likely to be grown — very often in a simple clay flower pot beside the door, at the corner of a path or even on the windowsill. In a modern cottage garden it is nice to grow geraniums in the same way, although it would be most appropriate to confine your selection to red, white or soft pink in order to blend with the subtle, hazy shades of the cottage flowers of summer.

Herbs

MANY OF THE PLANTS that we have already mentioned could be described as herbs in the context of the traditional cottage garden because they were employed for such a variety of uses in cooking, preserving and the treatment of everyday ailments. However, cottagers would also have grown those plants which we know and recognize as culinary herbs and which would, as such, be most appealing to modern gardeners.

Rosemary is an attractive shrub as well as a useful herb; here its grey foliage contrasts with the golden bloom of Genista hispanica

The applications to which we would put the cottage herbs now are mainly in cooking or flavouring and perhaps making perfumed sachets, pomanders and pot-pourri. Their medical applications, both ancient and modern, are interesting to read about, and therefore we pass on, as a matter of interest, some of the most widely recognized uses of the cottage herbs in the treatment of everyday coughs, colds, cuts and bruises. However, medical herbalism demands a degree of knowledge quite beyond the scope of a gardening book, and before dabbling it would be sensible to study a good modern herbal such as Grieve's.

For use in the kitchen, the cottage herbs can be picked fresh from the garden in spring and summer; in this state their flavour is fullest and most pungent, and the fresh leaves will keep for a few days if stored in an airtight container. For winter use, new, leafy stems should be picked before the plant flowers, and the leaves can either be thoroughly dried in a warm, dark place that is dry but well ventilated or can be blanched, allowed to cool and then frozen. When required for flavouring hot dishes, they can be used straight from the freezer, but once thawed they should not be refrozen.

In the garden, the majority of herbs like a sunny spot in light, well drained soil. They can, of course, be grown in pots or containers — on the

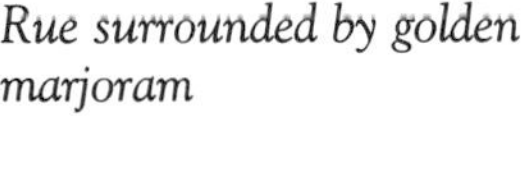

Rue surrounded by golden marjoram

windowsill as well as outdoors — or you could create a herb patch devoted to their cultivation. This could be most conveniently located quite close to the house, where you can enjoy the aromatic and ornamental qualities of the plants as well as being able to step outside and pick a bunch of herbs whenever you need them.

As we have seen, cottagers would often have a herb patch, but were also just as likely to grow the traditional culinary herbs in amongst flowering plants and, indeed, some herbs are just as well known as ornamental garden plants, and extremely useful in this context.

Three that come particularly to mind are rosemary, thyme and rue; all are very cottagey but at the same time are valued for their adaptability and their general appearance as garden plants.

Thyme is a hardy evergreen, and there is a tremendous range of varieties to give variation of leaf and flower colouring, as well as form. It is well worth growing half a dozen different thymes, or even more, in a cottage garden. As garden plants, the most useful are *Thymus serpyllum* (wild thyme) and its cultivars; the plants have grey-green leaves and tiny flowers ranging in colour from deep to pale pink, and white. As a low-growing ground cover it is quite superb, withstanding drought, compaction and treading; in dry, exposed positions it will flourish where little else will grow at all, making it invaluable for stony areas, dry walls, paths and between paving.

The two best culinary thymes, the lemon scented *T. x citriodorus* and the common *T. vulgaris*, are also good garden plants. There are some lovely varieties of lemon scented thyme, including the glowing golden 'Aureus' and the pale green variegated white 'Silver Queen', and the clusters of mauve flowers of the common thyme are an attractive and familiar feature of the plant, appearing in June.

As a herb, thyme is not only a pleasing flavouring for stuffings and stews; it is one of the ingredients in Benedictine liqueur and essence of thyme is used in the perfume and cosmetic industry. Medicinally, fragrant thymol oil acts as antiseptic, tonic and antispasmodic, and thyme tea was traditionally taken for colic, colds and fevers.

Rosemary — the very name is prettily old-fashioned and, like lavender, evocative of a warmly perfumed sunny afternoon in a country garden. *Rosmarinus officinalis* is a good bushy, evergreen shrub that grows 5–6 feet (1.5–2 m) tall with a spread of 4–5 feet (1.2–1.5 m), and can be grown as an individual specimen or to make a fine hedge. The most suitable for hedging is 'Miss Jessop's Variety'; plants should be placed 2 feet (60 cm) apart, and the hedge can be trimmed in spring before flowering in May–June.

The ancient Greeks believed that rosemary strengthened the memory, and it became the emblem of remembrance, love and friendship at christenings, weddings and funerals. In its more practical applications, oil of rosemary is used not only to treat digestive and nervous disorders, but also as an ingredient in hair lotions, and it is said that a tea made up from the dried leaves, cooled and mixed with borax, makes an effective hair wash to prevent scurf and dandruff. In cooking, the strong, pungent aroma goes particularly well with meat; (try laying a few sprigs on lamb or chicken whilst it is cooking on a barbecue).

Rue (*Ruta graveolens*) is one of the oldest of the traditional cottage plants, having been introduced by the Romans. It, too, is a useful shrub — a small semi-evergreen plant of dense habit with glaucous, blue-grey leaves that have an almost luminous quality, and mustard yellow flowers in summer. The sharp colour contrast and bitter, acrid taste have perhaps contributed to rue's symbolism of regret, sorrow and repentance — an impression reinforced by the fact that in the late eighteenth century the dried leaves of rue were spread on the floors of prisons and courtrooms as a disinfectant against typhus or 'gaol fever'. It is certainly a natural pesticide and fumigant; bundles of the plant hung in the house, or a tea sprayed on to plants are said to keep away insects.

Although these three are especially ornamental, there is in addition a whole host of traditional cottage herbs that are still worth growing. The following all thrive in full sun in a light, well-drained soil: sweet basil, borage, catnep, chamomile, chicory, cotton lavender, dill, good King Henry, hyssop, lady's mantle, melissa or lemon balm, marjoram, meadowsweet, myrtle, sage and southernwood. A number of these are readily available as young plants from garden centres, and some can be grown from seed; all are available from the many specialist herb nurseries that now exist around the country, many of whom supply by mail order.

Sweet basil is one herb that is especially suitable to grow from seed because, although a perennial, it is not hardy and is therefore treated as an annual plant in this country. Seed can be sown indoors or out in May, or plants set out during June, growing 2–3 feet (60–90 cm) tall with light green, aromatic leaves that are softly hairy. They originated in tropical Asia, Africa and the Pacific Islands and in India sweet basil is cherished by Hindu households as the protector of the spirit of the family. It is used in India as a powerful, pungent flavouring in curries and in Italy is widely added to egg, cheese, fish and tomato dishes. It was introduced to Britain in the mid sixteenth century, and as well as its culinary applications, the powdered leaves were taken as snuff and as a relief from headaches.

Borage, too, is a hardy annual that makes quite a large plant, having silvery-grey hairy leaves and blue, star-shaped flowers that bloom from June to October. It is a native to western Mediterranean countries, and in ancient Greece its invigorating, tonic effect gave it a reputation as the herb of courage. The fresh leaves and flowers have a flavour like cucumber, and are very refreshing in salads and drinks.

Catnep is a much less exotic herb; a native perennial, its natural habitat is the humble hedgerow or waste ground, especially on chalky soils, so in the garden it is useful for areas of poor soil that are inclined to drought. As the name suggests, its aromatic odour has a strange attraction for cats; tiny glands on the plant seem to release the odour when touched or rubbed, sending cats into an oblivious euphoria. An infusion of the leaves is said to be a soothing and sedative drink for colds, stress and restlessness.

Hyssop, an aromatic evergreen shrub

Chamomile is another perennial and a native of sandy soils; its light green, finely cut leaves make it an attractive, aromatic garden plant that is capable of creeping or trailing to form, eventually, a dense mat of growth that can withstand light pedestrian traffic. A chamomile lawn takes a little while to establish, but can be a most appealing and traditional feature — especially for a front garden — and an intriguing change from grass.

As for the medicinal application of chamomile, it is hard to dissociate the plant from poor Peter Rabbit, who was sent to bed with chamomile tea when suffering from over-indulgence in Mr McGregor's vegetable garden. The tea is certainly reputed for its ability to relieve indigestion and for improving the appetite. Interestingly, chamomile is also a constituent in cosmetics and the dried flowers produce a bright yellow dye.

The flowers of chicory also produce a dye — in this case blue, from the blooms that appear between July and September. However, it is the leaves of this easily grown native perennial that are most valuable for their use in salads (far superior to dandelion leaves, which they somewhat resemble) and the root is well known as a caffeine-free coffee substitute. Chicory is much more widely grown on the Continent than in Britain, although in 1788 there was an attempt to introduce it here as a fodder for livestock. Nevertheless, it is still worthy of consideration by modern cottage gardeners who like to add something a little different to salads.

The herb dill has some intriguing associations; having been introduced to Britain from the Mediterranean by the Romans, it was used by magicians in the Middle Ages as part of their spells and charms against witchcraft. The name actually comes from the old Norse word, *dilla* meaning to lull, because it was found to be effective against insomnia and generally calming and soothing.

An attractive variegated sage, Salvia officinalis *'Icterina'*

The herb has a gentle fragrance and is ideal for salads, soups, sauces or fish, and the seeds, too, can be used although they have a stronger, bitter taste. Dill vinegar is made by soaking the seeds in vinegar for a few days before using, and the seeds have also been used in gripe water, to treat wind in babies.

To Pickle cucumbers in Dill

Gather the tops of the ripest dill and cover the bottom of the vessel, and lay a layer of cucumbers and another of dill till you have filled the vessel within a handful of the top. Then take as much water as you think will fill the vessel and mix it with salt and a quarter of a pound of allom to a gallon of water and poure it on them and press them down with a stone on them and keep them covered close. For that use I think the water will be best boyl'd and cold, which will keep longer sweet, or if you like not this pickle, doe it with water, salt and white wine vinegar, or (if you please) pour the water and salt on them scalding hot which will make them ready to use the sooner.

from recipe book of Joseph Cooper, Cook to Charles I, 1640

The name of good King Henry is just as interesting as the plant; it was apparently given in order to distinguish the herb from another of similar appearance but poisonous qualities, known as bad Henry. At the turn of the century, good King Henry was regularly grown as a vegetable in Suffolk and Lincolnshire, where it was eaten in place of spinach, for the flavour is similar although less pronounced. The plant is also known for its excellent remedial qualities for indigestion.

Lady's mantle is another herb with an appealing name and an ancient reputation. The name apparently derives from the fact that the tea (1–2 teaspoons of lady's mantle per cup of boiling water) was thought to be extremely helpful for women if taken twice daily during pregnancy and for two weeks after giving birth. It was also considered to be one of the best herbs for treating wounds because of its drying and binding properties. The plant is a hardy herbaceous perennial that is easy to grow; it should be planted between October and March in a sunny or partially shady position, and has most attractive foliage and light yellow flowers.

The word melissa is Greek for honey bee, and as well as its common name of lemon balm, melissa was also known as 'bee herb', in acknowledgement of the ancient belief that bees would not stray or lose their way from the hive if the plant grew close to it. Melissa can be added to many foods and its chopped leaves can be used as a lemon substitute, but its delicate lemon flavour is best brought out in drinks, and especially melissa tea, which helps relaxation and is said to dispel headaches and tiredness.

Melissa Tea
1 teaspoon lemon balm leaves per cup and 1 for the pot. Place leaves, whole or freshly crushed, in warmed but dried cups or teapot. Pour boiling water over herbs; allow to steep for 3–5 minutes only; strain.

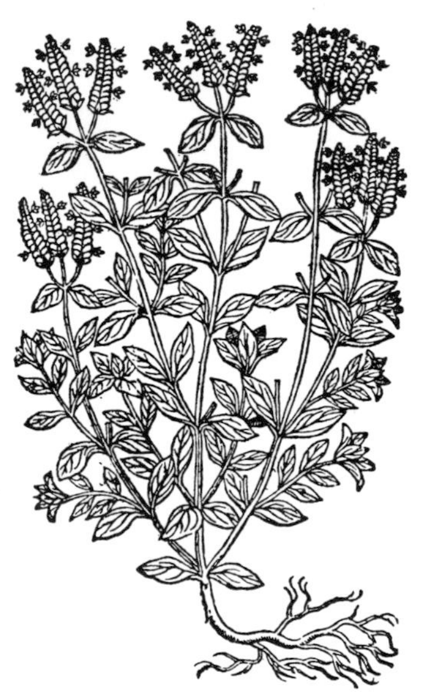

Common marjoram (*Origanum vulgare*) is a hardy perennial that grows 12–18 inches (30–45 cm) tall and bears pink flowers in July and August. It is an ancient herb with many traditional uses; the flowering tops produce a dye that was used by country people to dye woollen cloth purple and linen a reddish brown. The tops can also be used in beer, to preserve it and lend an aromatic flavour and were very much in demand for ale brewing before the introduction of hops.

Medicinally, a tea made from the fresh plant is said to relieve nervous headache and in food marjoram is used extensively in Italian cuisine, including the Neapolitan pizza. It is excellent for use on grilled meats or roasts, and in soup, sauces, egg, cheese or tomato dishes.

Sweet marjoram (*Origanum marjoram*) is one of the most important culinary herbs, with a flavour similar to that of thyme but sweeter and more fragrant. The herb dries well and is most suitable for quick freezing, making it available all year round.

The notion of freezing herbs was quite beyond the experience of cottagers, but then the notion of using marjoram as an important ingredient in the ceremony described in 'Halliwell's Popular Rhymes & Superstitions' is quite beyond our experience today!

> On St. Luke's Day says Mother Bunch take marigold flowers, a sprig of marjoram, thyme and a little wormwood; dry them before a fire, rub them to powder, then sift it through a fine piece of lawn, and simmer it over a slow fire, adding a small quantity of virgin honey and vinegar. Anoint yourself with this when you go to bed, saying the following lines three times and you will dream of your future partner 'that is to be':
> St. Luke, St. Luke, be kind to me,
> In dreams let me my true love see.
> If a girl desires to obtain this information, let her seek for a green peascod in which there are full 9 peas, and write on a piece of paper —
> Come in, my dear,
> And do not fear;
> which paper she must enclose in the peascod, and lay it under the door,
> The first person who comes into the room will be her husband.

Myrtle (*Myrtus communis*) is a traditional cottage evergreen shrub with glossy, aromatic leaves. As a garden plant, myrtle can reach 8–10 feet (2.5–3 m) tall with an equal spread, but it originated in Mediterranean regions and is only hardy in sheltered parts of the south and west of Britain. As a herb, it is used widely in Italian salami, and in stuffings and sausages, as well as for enhancing the flavour of beans and peas.

The strong flavour of sage is probably familiar to most people for its use with roast meat, gravies and in stuffing. However, it has also long been valued for its wide ranging medicinal qualities; indeed, the name derives from the Latin *salvere* — to be saved, in reference to its curative properties — and in the United States it is still listed as an official medicine, valued for its treatment of mouth and throat infections. In his Herball, Gerard was extremely enthusiastic about the effectiveness of sage in treating a whole string of afflictions and added: 'No man needs to doubt the wholesomeness of Sage Ale, being brewed as it should be, with Sage, Scabious, Betony, Spikenard, Squinanth, and Fennell seeds.'

Southernwood was another very traditional cottage herb, and was also known as lad's love, for sprigs would be included in lovers' posies. The leaves have a lemony perfume, and are said to be disagreeable to insects; for this reason, they were often made into pot-pourri and placed amongst clothes to deter moths and fleas — hence the French name of *garde-robe*. They were also placed under the pillow to alleviate sleeplessness.

Most people can find a dry, sunny spot for herbs somewhere in the garden — or indeed several locations — for it is in these conditions that all the herbs mentioned so far will flourish. However, there are some important cottage herbs that prefer damper or shadier conditions — notably angelica, chives, mint and parsley.

Angelica is a native of stream banks, damp meadows and hedgerows; the tall, stout, hairy plant grows from 3–8 feet (1–2.5 m) high and the whole plant is aromatic — purple-tinged stem, large, dark green leaves and white flowers tinted pink, which are borne in large umbells. Young plants can be set out in spring in a damp situation in sun or partial shade, but you should allow 4 feet (1.2 m) between them. Angelica is a short-lived perennial; plants may take from two to five years to flower, and then die, but they do self seed.

Angelica was said to be named after the archangel Michael, and it was held in high esteem as a protection against evil spirits and witchcraft. Various old writers praise its effectiveness as a cure for almost every conceivable ailment, including bronchitis, asthma and colds. In China the root is eaten as a painkiller and the whole plant is reputed to build up resistance to infection, having been much used in times of plague. It is recommended as a bath additive or a hot tea to calm the nerves, but is probably most familiar now for its candied leaf stalks and young stems.

Chives are native perennial bulbous plants, and being a relative of the onion, have narrow grass-like leaves in clumps. They like a medium to heavy soil, and the flowers can be removed when they appear, to encourage more leafy growth.

Borage wtih chives which have been allowed to bloom as an edging plant to a border

The chive contains a pungent, volatile oil rich in sulphur, which produces the distinctive, oniony smell and taste. The plant is mildly antiseptic and regarded as a tonic and blood purifier. The freshly chopped leaves are a pleasing addition to any salad dish or savoury recipe.

(left) Large, showy angelica plants combine with other foliage plants creating a pleasing combination of shapes and colours

Chive Butter
2 tablespoons chopped fresh chives
500 g (1 lb) butter
1 pinch salt (optional)
Bring the butter to room temperature, and whip in the chives and salt. Refrigerate and serve with hot rolls, hot biscuits, or baked potatoes.

Many species of mint (*mentha*) were as familiar to cottage gardeners as they are today, but they all share a common problem as garden plants — a tendency to invasiveness, their underground runners quite quickly taking over a large area if left unchecked. In order to prevent this, the roots should be contained; in a small garden, you could grow plants in large, bottomless tubs or pots (18 inches/45 cm deep) and submerge them in the soil, or you could bury a strip of corrugated plastic to a similar depth to cordon off a larger area.

Spearmint (*Mentha spicata*) is the most common garden mint, and most familiar for making traditional mint sauce as an accompaniment to lamb; mint jelly is also good, and can be made by steeping mint leaves in apple jelly or in various kinds of gelatine.

I have heard the pigeons of
the Seven Woods
Make their faint thunder,
and the garden bees
Hum in the lime-tree flowers
W. B. Yeats

Peppermint (M. *piperita*) has been extensively cultivated for centuries for oil of peppermint for use as a flavouring, but also as a very important medicinal agent, especially for all manner of complaints of the stomach and digestive system. However, it was 'Pennyroyal' (M. *pulegium*) that was probably most familiar in cottage gardens, being an old-fashioned remedy for colds, indigestion, depression, headache and rheumatism. 'Pennyroyal' is also said to have water purifying qualities, and in early voyages of exploration sailors used the herb to purify stale drinking water during long periods at sea. Although it is little used in the kitchen now, it is still an essential ingredient in north country black puddings.

Parsley is another common herb, just as familiar as mint, and the curly leaved variety can be an attractive addition to the garden. It is most easily grown as an annual in sun or partial shade, and seeds can be sown outdoors between February and June. Plants will go on for a second year, but the leaves are not quite as good. If you leave plants for a second year, be sure to remove the yellowy flowers as soon as they appear. The uses of parsley leaves are familiar, but it is also worth noting that they are rich in vitamins A, B and C.

So, both their value as foods and flavourings and the quality of many as ornamental plants make herbs well worth growing, even if you would not want to plant quite as many different types as cottagers might have done, nor dream of using them for quite such a range of applications!

Fennel

Traditional Recipe for **Aromatic Herbaceous Seasoning**

Take the nutmegs and mace 1 oz each, of cloves and peppercorns 2 oz each, 1 oz of dried bay-leaves, 3 oz of basil, the same for Marjoram, 2 oz of winter savoury and 3 oz of thyme, $\frac{1}{2}$ oz of cayenne pepper, the same of grated lemon peel and 2 cloves of garlic; all these ingredients must be well pulverized in a mortar, and sifted through a fine wire sieve, and put away in dry corked bottles for use.

Fruit

What wond'rous life is this I lead!
Ripe apples drop about my head;
The luscious clusters of the vine
Upon my mouth do crush their wine;
The nectarine and curious peach,
Into my hands themselves do reach;
Stumbling on melons, as I pass,
Insnar'd with flowers, I fall on grass.

'The Garden'
by Andrew Marvell

IN THE COTTAGE GARDEN, fruit and vegetables were vital. The garden was the major source of fresh food for the family, and it was essential to be as near self-sufficient as possible. Life is so different today that it is foolish to suggest that modern gardeners would wish to base the selection of vegetables they grow on the needs of the Victorian rural family. So, if your modern cottage garden includes a vegetable patch, then the choice of produce must be your own.

However, when it comes to fruit, it is worth noting not only the surprisingly wide range of traditional cottage gardens, but also considering the plants as garden plants in their own right before you banish them to a utility-style plot at the end of the garden.

As we mentioned when considering design, any tree must be regarded as a major feature of the garden layout, and fruit trees are no exception. They can create interest above eye-level and offer leafy shade and a sense of shelter, as well as producing a crop of luscious fruit, but they should be planted at a suitable distance from the house and in a sunny, open position.

Of course, apple trees are most traditional and are rather attractive trees with their soft, springtime blossom, fresh summer leaves and satisfying burden of ripening fruit. The variety you choose will depend on whether you want a dessert or cooker, and your preference for taste, but you should remember that most must be cross-pollinated by a different variety if they are to set fruit really well. If you have room for only one tree, either choose one that complements any growing in neighbouring gardens or go for one of the few self-fertile apples — for dessert, 'Ellison's Orange' and 'Laxton's Superb' and for cooking, 'Grenadier'.

A large garden will allow space for a standard tree, which usually has a 6 foot (2 m) clear stem, but a half-standard obviously makes a slightly smaller tree and for tiny gardens a bush is a very practical alternative. With a stem of only 2–3 feet (60–90 cm) and an open-centred head of branches, a bush fruit tree will produce a crop more quickly than standards and is much more accessible for picking and pruning.

The other fruit trees that were most frequently grown in cottage gardens were plums and, perhaps surprisingly, peaches. Plums are easy to grow;

WOOD AVENS.
GEUM URBANUM
BRAMBLE
BLACKBERRY.
BLACK-BERRY.
BRAMBLE
RUBUS
DISCOLOR.
WATER AVENS.
GEUM RIVALE
RUBUS
RHAMNIFOLIUS.

Gooseberries were a cottage garden favourite

Victoria plums

they benefit from the addition of lime to the soil when planting, but once established require hardly any pruning and are rarely troubled with pests and diseases. The most familiar and traditional variety is 'Victoria'; the fruit is large and bright red and is suitable for both dessert and cooking and bottling. It has the additional benefit of being self-fertile.

Peaches are often thought of as being rather exotic and too tender to be grown in British gardens. However, they will thrive and fruit in all but the coldest areas if carefully sited and tended, and you can grow a peach either as a fan-trained tree, the branches spreading flat against a warm, sunny wall, or as a bush in an open position, although it is important to have a well-drained soil containing lime. The most hardy and reliable variety is 'Peregrine', which produces juicy, well-flavoured fruit from mid-August onwards.

Cottagers grew soft fruit in amongst the flowers, and when you look at the bushy growth of currants and gooseberries, the pleasing ground cover effect of strawberries, the dense hedging of blackberries and the lush, spreading leaves of rhubarb, it is not difficult to see why.

Both red and blackcurrants were grown, and both could be treated as shrubs in the modern cottage garden, growing amongst perennials and annuals. They make good sized bushes with attractive, fresh green foliage; a sunny position is ideal, with protection from wind, and a rich, fertile soil will produce the best results. Bushes can be planted between October and March, but autumn is ideal. Good varieties of redcurrant are 'Laxton's No. 1' and 'Red Lake' and popular blackcurrants include 'Baldwin', 'Boskoop Giant' and 'Wellington XXX'.

Gooseberries are very traditional — especially the dessert variety 'Leveller' which is widely grown today. Plants can be treated in much the

Autumn is over the long
leaves that love us,
And over the mice in the
barley sheaves;
Yellow the leaves of the
rowan above us,
And yellow the wet wild-
strawberry leaves
W. B. Yeats

same way as currants, but they are prone to send up suckers from below ground level, and these should be removed as soon as they appear.

Blackberries or brambles would, of course, hardly have to be invited into a country garden. It is rather more a question of trying to control their vigorous growth, although they can be useful for bulking up an informal hedge into a really dense screen. The cultivated hybrids like 'Himalayan Giant' and 'Oregon Thornless' will produce more fruit than the wild blackberries, but all need support in the form of a fence or wall.

Rhubarb is a great space filler in a bed or border, and the massive leaves can make quite a pleasing contrast with more delicate flowers. Plants prefer a rich soil in an open position; water well in the first season after planting, and then keep watered during dry weather. Feed occasionally with a general fertilizer in spring and summer and remove any flower stems as they appear.

Strawberries are not only a delicious fruit and as essential to the English summer as hollyhocks and roses, but they also make a rather good plant for pots or ground cover. As well as the summer fruiting varieties, you could grow perpetual strawberries, which fruit from June through to the first frosts (the main crop being picked in August–September). Good varieties are 'Rabunda' and 'Gento'.

Alpine strawberries also produce small fruits right through the summer. The variety most usually available is 'Baron Solemacher' and it is particularly in the spirit of the cottage garden, for plants can be grown as an edging to the front of larger plants, and are even tolerant of shade.

Plant check-list

Shrubs

Buddleia davidii — (Butterfly Bush). Height and spread to 10 ft (3 m) or more. A vigorous shrub. Flowers, fragrant, lilac-pink with a yellow eye, in dense clusters, 10–12 ins (25–30 cm) long. Any soil in sun.

Buxus sempervirens — (Box). Native. Height to 10 ft (3 m). Spread 4–6 ft (1.25–2 m). A slow growing shrub of bushy habit. Leaves, dark green, glossy. Flowers, inconspicious, honey-scented. April. Any soil in sun or part shade.

Chaenomeles speciosa — (Japanese quince. Japonica). Height 6–12 ft (2–4 m) spreading. Leaves, dark green, glossy. Flowers in shades of red, 2 ins (5 cm) wide, in clusters. January–April. Fruit, yellow-green, fragrant. Any soil, sun or part shade. Can be trained on walls.

Cotoneaster microphyllus — Height 18 ins (45 cm). Spread 6–8 ft (2–2.5 m). Evergreen, dwarf shrub. Leaves, dark green, glossy. Flowers white, ⅓ in (10 mm) across. May–June. Berries scarlet. Any soil in sun or part shade.

Daphne mezereum — (Mezereon). Height 2–5 ft (60–150 cm). Spread to 4 ft (120 cm). Flowers, fragrant, red-purple to purple-pink, in dense clusters on leafless stems.
Variety
'Alba'. White flowers and berries. Any well-drained soil in sun or part shade.

Deutzia gracilis — Height 2–3 ft (60–90 cm). Spread 4–6 ft (1.25–2 m). Flowers white. Star-shaped in panicles 3 ins (7.5 cm) long. June. A well-drained soil in sun or part shade.

Fuchsia magellanica — 'Riccartonii'. Height 4–8 ft (1.25–2.5 m). Spread to 4 ft (120 cm). A bushy, hardy fuchsia. Flowers, red sepals, purple petals, 1½–2 ins (4–5 cm) long. July–August. Any well-drained humus-rich soil. Sun or part shade.

Hypericum androsaemum — (Tutsan). Native. Height 2–3 ft (60–90 cm). Leaves aromatic when crushed. Flowers yellow. June–August. Berries red, turning blue-black. A damp situation in part shade is best.

Hypericum calycinum	(Rose of Sharon). Height 12–18 ins (30–45 cm). Plant vigorous, spreading. Leaves bright green, oval. Flowers golden-yellow. 2–3 inches (5–7.5 cm) across. June–September. Any soil, sun or part shade.
Hypericum x inodorum	'Elstead'. Height to 4 ft (120 cm). Flowers pale yellow. July–October. Berries red, in large clusters. A fertile, well-drained soil in sun or part shade.
Kerria japonica	Height and spread 4–6 ft (1.25–2 m). Leaves light green, toothed. Flowers yellow-orange, 1½ ins (4 cm) across. April–May. Any soil, in sun or part shade.
Lavandula spica	'Munstead'. Height 1½–2 ft (45–60 cm). Leaves silvery-grey. Flowers blue in spikes. July. A well-drained soil in sun. *Variety* 'Twickel Purple'
Philadelphus	'Belle Etoile'. A compact shrub. Height to 6 ft (2 m). Flowers 2 ins (5 cm) wide, fragrant. Any well-drained soil in sun or part shade.
Philadelphus coronarius	'Aureus'. Height 6–9 ft (2–3 m). Young foliage bright golden-yellow, turning green-yellow. In part or full shade.
Philadelphus	'Manteau d' Hermine'. Height 2–4 ft (60–120 cm). A compact shrub. Flowers creamy-white, double, fragrant. Any well-drained soil in sun or part shade.
Rhododendron	Enormous range of species and cultivars. All are lime-hating and require an acid sandy or peaty soil, and prefer partial shade. Recommended for cottage gardens: 'Pink Pearl', 'Fastuosum Flore Pleno' (pale bluish mauve) both 6 x 4 ft (2 x 1.2 m) and 'Blue Diamond', 'Bluebird', 'Pink Drift'.
Ribes sanguineum	'King Edward VII'. Height 6–9 ft (2–3 m). Spread 5–7 ft (1.5–2 m). Leaves heart-shaped, dark green. Flowers crimson. March–May. 2–4 ins (5–10 cm) long. Any well-drained soil in sun or part shade.
Symphoricarpus albus	(Snowberry). Height 5–7 ft (1.5–2 m). Spread 7–8 ft (2 m). Leaves broadly-oval, green. Flowers small, pink. July–September. Berries white, ½ in (13 mm) across. October–February. A well-drained soil in sun or part shade.
Syringa vulgaris	(Common Lilac). Height 8–12 ft (2–4 m). Spread 5–10 ft (1.5–3 m). Leaves heart-shaped or oval. Flowers lilac, fragrant in panicles, 6–10 ins (15–25 cm) long. May–June. *Variety* 'Maud Notcutt'. Large, single white flowers. May. A fertile soil in sun or part shade.
Vinca minor	Low, spreading habit. Leaves dark green, glossy, evergreen. Flowers blue, 1 in (2.5 cm) across. March–July, often until October. Any well-drained soil in part shade.

Roses (with dates of introduction)

Rosa alba	Vigorous, erect shrub with greyish green leaves. Smooth stems with few large prickles. Oval hips. Flowers once in summer. Flower colours white to pink. *Varieties*: *R. alba semi-plena*. 'White Rose of York'. Flowers semi-double, white, midsummer *R. alba*. 'Great Maiden's Blush'. Flowers white blushed pink with beautiful scent. Midsummer. Before 15th century.
Rosa gallica	Compact shrubs with pointed leaves. Stems covered in hairy bristles. Flowers pink to deep red, maroons, mauves. *Varieties*: *R. gallica officinalis*. 'Red Rose of York' or 'Apothecary's Rose'. Bushy growth. Semi-double light crimson flowers with yellow stamens. Midsummer. *R. gallica Versicolor*. 'Rosa Mundi'. Gorgeous crimson flowers splashed and striped white. Midsummer. Before 16th century.
R. damascena	Open, prickly growth. Open-shaped flowers, superb perfume. Long narrow hips. *Variety*: 'York and Lancaster'. Flowers pink-white. Midsummer.
R. centifolia	'Cabbage Rose'. Open growth, large, rounded leaves. Full, double blooms white to pink. Midsummer. Plant 5 × 4ft (150 × 120 cm).
Moss Roses	Similar characteristics to parent *R. centifolia*, but with sticky, bristly 'moss' covering branches, flower stalks and sepals. *Variety*: 'Nuits de Young'. Plant 5 × 3ft (150 × 90 cm). Deep maroon-purple flowers with yellow stamens. 1851.
R. rubiginosa	'Sweet Briar' or 'Eglantine'. Single pale pink blooms, lovely fragrance. Midsummer. Bright red oval hips. Vigorous — good for a hedge. Plant 8 × 8ft (2.5 × 2.5 m).
R. spinosissima	'Scotch Briar'. Dense, straight, upright branches with tiny leaves and thorns. Mass of small white or pink flowers. Maroon-black hips. Spreads by suckering.
R. moyesii	Large bush with erect branches, fine foliage, single red blooms. Midsummer. Superb long, flagon-shaped hips in early autumn. *Variety*: 'Geranium'. More moderate growth. Fresh green leaves, red flowers. Midsummer. 1938.
R. chinensis	China roses prefer a warm, sunny position. Flower in early June then right into autumn. 'Old Blush China'. Crimson buds, soft pink semi-double flowers.
R. bourboniana	Bourbon roses are vigorous; repeat flowering. 'Boule de Neige'. Plant 6 × 4ft (180 × 120 cm). Flowers white, full, rounded, camellia-like.

Hybrid perpetuals	'Reine des Violettes'. Lilac-purple blooms, delicious scent. 6 × 5ft (180 × 150 cm). 1860. 'Ulrich Brunner'. Large rosy-like blooms, strong fragrance. 6 × 4 ft (180 × 120 cm). 1882.
Hybrid Musk	'Penelope'. Sturdy, branching shrub. Mass of semi-double pink flowers, musk scented. Good hips. Repeat flowering. 1924.
Modern repeat flowering shrubs:	'Angelina'. Rich pink blooms with white shaded centre, prominent yellow stamens. 1975. 'Ballerina'. Huge clusters pale pink single blooms with white eye. 3–4ft tall (90–120 cm). Good for hedge. 1937. 'Lavender Lassie'. Ruffled, fragrant pink blooms in clusters. 4ft tall. 1960. 'The Fairy'. Polyantha type with clusters of tiny pink rosettes. Low and spreading. 1932. 'Snow Carpet'. Miniature ground cover rose with mass of white blooms. 1980.

Climbing and Rambling Roses

Alberic Barbier	Full, creamy yellow blooms, apple scented. Rambler reaches 25ft (8 m). Midsummer. 1900.
Albertine	Bushy, sprawling rambler with dark, glossy foliage. Reaches 18ft (6 m). Very fragrant flowers two-tone pink. 1921.
R. banksiae	Vigorous rambler reaches 25ft (8 m). Rather tender and needs sunny position. Fragrant white flowers in spring. Evergreen foliage. *Variety* 'Lutea'. Double yellow. 1824.
Dorothy Perkins	Typical cottage rambling rose. Summer flowering. Pink blooms borne in large clusters. 1901.
Aloha	Repeat flowering climber of moderate growth. Large double flowers coral-pink. Can be grown on a north wall. 1949.
Schoolgirl	Beautiful fragrant apricot-copper blooms shaded pink. Repeat flowering. Vigorous grower. 1964.
Zephirine Drouhin	Bourbon type climber. Sweetly fragrant, vivid pink blooms. Repeat flowering. Thornless. Grows to 15ft (5 m). 1868.

Climbing plants

Clematis x jackmanii	(C. *lanuginosa x c. viticella*). Height 12–16 ft (4–5 m). Leaves, pinnate. Flowers large, 12 ins (30 cm) across, 4 petals, violet-purple. July–October. A well-drained soil with lime, in a sunny position. Shade base and roots from strong sunlight.

Hedera helix	'Goldheart'. Leaves green with a yellow-gold centre. Any soil in sun or shade. Excellent for ground and wall cover. *Varieties* 'Caenwoodiana' 'Hibernica'
Jasminum nudiflorum	(Winter Jasmine). Height to 10 ft (3 m). Leaves dark green. Flowers yellow, ½–1 in (13–25 mm) across. November–April. A well-drained soil in any situation. Needs support.
Jasminum officinale	(White Jasmine). Height 30 ft (10 m). A vigorous, hardy climber. Flower white, in long clusters. June–October. A well-drained soil in any position.
Lonicera periclymenum	(Honeysuckle, Woodbine). 'Belgica'. Height 10–20 ft (3–6 m). Flowers reddish-purple, turning to yellow. May–June and again in late summer. Any well-drained, humus-rich soil in sun or shade.
Parthenocissus quinquefolia	(Virginia Creeper). Very tall growing. Self-clinging. Leaves turn crimson in autumn. Flowers inconspicious, green-yellow. May–June. Berries blue-black. A fertile, humus-rich soil in sun or shade.
Vitis coignetiae	(Japanese Vine). Very tall. Leaves 3–5 lobes, green, in Autumn turning yellow, orange-red and purple-crimson. Flowers green in panicles, 3 ins (7.5 cm) long. Berries black. Inedible. A fertile, humus-rich soil. In sun or shade.

Perennial plants

Achillea millifolium	(Yarrow). Native. Height 1–2 ft (30–60 cm). Plant creeping, leaves finely divided, deep green. Flowers white or pink. June–Sept. Any soil in sun or part shade.
Ajuga reptans	(Bugle). Native. Height 4–12 ins (10–30 cm). Flowers blue, borne on short spikes. May–July. Good ground cover plant in sun or part shade.
Alyssum saxatile	(Gold Dust). Height 9–12 ins (23–30 cm). Leaves grey-green. Flowers golden-yellow in dense corymbs. April–June. Sunny situation. *Variety* 'Citrinum'. Flowers lemon-gold.
Aquilegia vulgaris	(Columbine). Native. Height 1–2 ft (30–60 cm). Leaves grey-green. Flowers short-spurred. Variable, blue, pink or white. May–June. Sun or part shade. *Varieties* 'Biedermeier'. Dense clusters of variously coloured flowers. 'Mrs. Scott-Elliot's Strain'. Long-spurred hybrid. Height 3 ft (1 m). Leaves pale green. Flowers cream, yellow, pink, red, crimson or blue. May–June.

Arabis caucasica	'Flore pleno'. Height 6–9 ins (15–23 cm). Leaves grey-green. Flowers double white. Feb–June. Prefers a well-drained soil in sun or part shade. *Variety* 'Rosea grandiflora'. Flowers deep rose pink.
Armeria maritima	(Thrift. Sea Pink). Native. Height 6–12 ins (15–30 cm). Leaves green and narrow, forming hummocks 12 ins (30 cm) across. Pink flowered heads. May–July. Sunny situation in a well-drained soil. *Variety* 'Vindictive'. Flowers rich crimson-red.
Aster amellus	'King George'. (Starwort). Height 18–24 ins (45–60 cm). Leaves grey-green. Flowers 2–3 ins (5–7.5 cm) across, violet-blue. August–Sept. Light, well-drained soil in a sunny situation. Excellent as cut flowers.
Aster novi-belgii	(Michaelmas Daisy). Height to 3 ft (1 m). Flowers numerous, approx 1 in (2.5 cm) across. Bright blue-violet. Sept–October. There are now many varieties of this species available.
Astilbe x arendsii	'Fanal'. Height 2–3 ft (60–90 cm). Attractive deep green foliage. The tiny dark red flowers are borne on dense pyramidal panicles between June and August. Requires a permanently moist root run in sun or part shade. Ideal as a pondside plant. *Varieties* 'Hyacinth'. Flowers rose-pink. 'White Gloria'. Flowers white.
Astrantia major	Height 2–3 ft (60–90 cm). Leaves green mostly basal. Pinkish star-like flowers 1 in (2.5 cm) across with similarly coloured bracts. June–July. Sun or part shade.
Aubrieta deltoidea	(Wall Cress). Head 3–4 ins (7.5–10 cm). Spreading to 2 ft (60 cm). Flowers purple to rose-lilac on short spikes. March–June. Sunny, well-drained situation. Useful for covering dry walls.
Bellis perennis	(Daisy). Height 1–4 ins (2.5–10 cm). Plants forming a dense mat. Flowers, white florets with a yellow centre. March–November. Good soil in sun or part shade.
Bergenia cordifolia	Height 12 ins (30 cm). Leaves soft fleshy, rounded or heart-shaped. Evergreen. Drooping heads of rose coloured flowers. March–April. Any soil in sun or part shade. *Variety* 'Purpurea'. Flowers pink-purple with purple tinged leaves.
Caltha palustris	(Marsh Marigold). Native. Height 1 ft (30 cm). Leaves deep green and rounded. Flowers cup-shaped, deep yellow, 1 in (2.5 cm across). April–May. Requires a wet situation in sun or part shade. Ideal in a boggy site or as a pond marginal.

Campanula carpatica	Height 9–12 ins (23–30 cm). Clump-forming. Flowers cup-shaped, 1½ ins (4 cm) wide. Variable from blue to purple. Also white. July–August. Any well-drained soil in sun or part shade.
Chrysanthemum maximum	Height 2½–3 ft (75 cm–90 cm). Leaves dark green. Flowers white, 3 ins across with a golden eye. June–August. Best in a sunny position. Excellent as cut flowers. There are now many named varieties. *Variety* 'Wirral Supreme'. Height 3 ft (1 m). Double white flowers.
Convallaria majalis	(Lily of the Valley). Native. Height 6–8 ins (15–20 cm). Spreading by submerged horizontal rhizomes. Leaves large, dark green. White bell-shaped scented flowers ¼ in (6 mm) long. April–May. Prefers a cool shaded position in a fertile soil.
Coreopsis grandiflora	Height 18–24 ins (45–60 cm). Leaves green, deeply cut. Flowers yellow, 2½ ins (6.5 cm) across. Excellent for cutting. Best in a fertile, well-drained soil in a sunny position. Withstands atmospheric pollution. There are many varieties.
Delphinium	Belladonna varieties. Height 3½–4½ ft (105–135 cm). Leaves green, deeply cut and segmented. Flowers, spurred in shades of blue, pink, purple and white on spikes. In a sheltered sunny position in deep fertile soil. *Recommended Belladonna varieties:* 'Blue Bees' 'Lodden Blue' 'Pink Sensation' Elatum variety (Dwarf): 'Blue Fountain'. Height 2½ ft (75 cm). Flowers shades of blue, mauve, white.
Dianthus	(Old-fashioned Pink. Cottage Pink). The Old-fashioned or Cottage Pink probably originated from Dianthus plumarius, a perennial native to Eastern Europe. Many old varieties and hybrids are derived from the parent plant and by crossing these with the perpetual flowering Carnation a new generation of Modern Pinks was introduced. The Old-fashioned or Cottage Pinks are easy to cultivate in a well-drained fertile soil. Lime is not necessary, but a good sunny position is important. The plants form tufted cushion-forming mats and their narrow pointed grey-green leaves are attractive all year round. Although hardy, they are short-lived perennials and should be replaced every 3–5 years, either from seed or cuttings. They are tolerant of atmospheric pollution. Height 10–15 ins (25–40 cm). There are many varieties and hybrids, with single or double flowers, which are often fragrant. *A few to be recommended are:* 'Bats Double' 'London Delight' 'Painted Lady' 'Damask Superb' 'Mrs. Sinkins' 'Sam Barlow' 'Laced Romeo' 'Paddington' 'Whiteladies'

Doronicum caucasicum	'Magnificum'. Height 18 ins (45 cm). Leaves bright green, coarsely toothed and heart-shaped. Flowers $2\frac{1}{2}$ ins (7.5 cm) across, yellow and long stalked. April–May. Regular dead-heading may produce a second show in the autumn. Sun or part shade in a deep moist fertile soil.
Doronicum plantagineum	Height 3 ft (1 m). Flowers 2–3 ins (5–7.5 cm) across. Golden yellow. April–June.
Epimedium grandiflorum	'Rose Queen'. Height 9–12 ins (23–30 cm). Best known for their coloured veining and tinted leaves in colours ranging from greens, gold, yellow, red and bronze. Flowers, spurred, crimson-carmine, 1 in (2.5 cm) long. May–June. A good ground cover plant for a moist situation in part shade, especially under trees.
Euphorbia epithymoides	(Spurge). Height 18 ins (45 cm). A bushy evergreen. Leaves oblong, green. Flowers insignificant, with bright yellow bracts, 3 ins (7.5 cm) across. April–May. A sunny position in well-drained soil. The milky juice exuded from any severed part of the plant is capable of producing dermatitis, though it is said to be excellent in the treatment and removal of warts.
Gaillardia aristata	Height 2–3 ft (60–90 cm). Leaves grey-green, basal and alternate. Flowers 3–4 ins (7.5–10 cm) across. Florets often tinted. Many varieties and colours. Excellent as cut flowers. A light well-drained soil in sun or part shade. *Varieties* 'Burgundy'. Wine-red. 'Dazzler'. Orange-yellow. 'Goblin'. Yellow and red, 9 ins (23 cm). 'Mandarin'. Orange and red. 'Wirral Flame'. Red and gold.
Geranium pratense	(Meadow Cranesbill). Native. Height $1\frac{1}{2}$–$2\frac{1}{2}$ ft (45–75 cm). Leaves 5–7 lobed, deeply divided. Flowers $\frac{1}{2}$–$1\frac{1}{2}$ ins (13–40 mm) across. Blue, violet-blue. Any well-drained soil in sun or part shade. *Varieties* 'Album' White 'Mrs. Kendall Clarke'. Blue.
Geum x borisii	Height 12 ins (30 cm). A hybrid between G. *reptans* and G. *bulgaricum*. Flowers orange-scarlet, 1 in (2.5 cm) across. May–Sept. Any soil enriched with humus, in sun or part shade.
Geum chiloense	'Mrs. Bradshaw'. Height $1\frac{1}{2}$–2 ft (45–60 cm). Semi-double flowers, scarlet.
Gypsophila paniculata	Height 3 ft (1 m). Leaves grey-green, grass-like. Flowers in loose panicles of single white flowers. June–August. Any well-drained soil in a sunny position.

Helleborous niger	(Christmas Rose). Height 1½ ft (45 cm). Leaves dark green, leathery and evergreen. Flowers white with golden anthers 1½–2 ins (4–5 cm) across. December–March. A deep well-drained soil in a moist situation. Protect blooms from severe frost.
Hemerocallis	(Day Lily) Garden hybrids. Height 2½–3 ft (75–90 cm). Leaves pale green, sword-shaped and arching. Flowers large 5–7 ins (13–18 cm) across. June–August. Fertile soil in sun or part shade. Numerous forms and colours. 'Black Magic'. Purple with a yellow throat. 'Golden Orchid'. Orange-yellow. 'Marion Vaughn'. Yellow with a green throat. 'Pink Prelude'. Pink.
Hosta	Attractive foliage, leaves broad, veined. Flowers in spikes. Excellent for moist shady conditions in a humus-enriched soil.
Hosta albo-marginata	Height 1–1½ ft (30–45 cm). Leaves, green with a white margin. Lilac flowers 2 ins (5 cm) long. July–August.
Hosta fortunei	'Albopicta'. Height 1½–2 ft (45–60 cm). Pale green leaves with broad yellow variegation, turning to glaucous-green. Flowers lilac, 1½ ins (4 cm) long. July–August. 'Aureo-marginata'. Height 2–3 ft (60–90 cm). Leaves broad, green with a gold margin. Flowers lilac, 1½ ins (4 cm) long. July–August.
Iberis sempervirens	'Snowflake'. (Candytuft). Height 6–9 ins (15–23 cm). Leaves dark green, narrow. Plant spreading, mat forming. Flowers white. May–June.
Iris foetidissima	(Stinking Iris). Native. Height 2–3 ft (60–90 cm). Leaves 1 in (2.5 cm) across, long, pointed. Foul smelling when crushed. Flowers purple-grey. Distinctive flower pod and scarlet seed in autumn. Excellent for dry chalky soils in sun or part shade.
Iris germanica	(London Flag). 2–4 ft (60–120 cm). Leaves grey-green, long, pointed. Evergreen. Flowers scented 3–4 ins (7.5–10 cm) across. May. Thin out rhizomes and replant every 3–5 years. Plant in full sun. Many varieties. 'Blue Shimmer' 'Gudrun'
Iris sibirica	Height 2–3½ ft (60–105 cm). Flowers 2½ ins (6.5 cm) across. Flowers, in shades of blue with white veining. June. Any soil in a sunny, preferably moist, position. The species is difficult to obtain as it hybridizes freely with its related species. Hybrids. Height to 3 ft (1 m). Flowers 3–4 ins (7.5–10 cm) across. 'Cambridge'. Pale Blue. 'Helen Astor'. Pink. 'Violet Flare' 'White Swirl'

Kniphofia uvaria — (Red Hot Poker). Height 3–5 ft (1–1.5 m). Leaves dark green, broad spreading. Flowers red, orange and yellow spikes. July–Sept. Any well-drained soil in sun.

Lathyrus latifolius — (Everlasting Pea). Height 6–10 ft (2–3 m). A vigorous climber that can be trained to supports in various positions. Leaves, dull green. Flowers 1 in (2.5 m) wide. Rose-purple. Also white. June–Sept. Any well-drained soil in full sun.

Lunaria rediviva — Height 3–3½ ft (90–105 cm). Short lived perennial. Plant bushy, erect with deep green oval leaves. Flowers white-pink. Fragrant. Any well-drained soil in sun or part shade.

Lupinus — Russell varieties. Height 2–3 ft (60–90 cm). Flowers borne on spikes. Many varieties with keel and stand petals in contrasting colours. Any soil (not too acid) in sun or part shade.

Varieties

'Blue Jacket' 'George Russell'
'Cherry Pie' 'Lilac Time'
'Freedom' 'Limelight'

Lychnis coronaria — (Dusty Miller. Rose Campion). Height 1½–2 ft (45–60 cm). Stem branching, silvery-grey. Leaves, woolly, oval. Flowers crimson or white. 1½ in (4 cm) across. July–Sept. Any well-drained soil in sun or part shade.

Monarda didyma — Varieties. (Horse Mint. Sweet Bergamot). Height 2–3 ft (60–90 cm). Leaves oval, hairy, aromatic. Flowers, dense heads, 2½–3 ins (6–7.5 cm) across. June–Sept. Humus-rich soil in a moist situation. Sun or part shade.

Varieties

'Blue stocking'
'Cambridge Scarlet'
'Croftway Pink'
'Pillar Box'
'Snow Maiden'

Nepeta mussinii — (*N. x faassenii*). A garden hybrid. Height 1–2 ft (30–60 cm). Leaves grey-green, narrowly oval. Flowers on spikes 6 ins (15 cm) long. Blue. May–Sept. Any well-drained soil in sun or part shade.

Paeonia lactiflora — (Peony). Height 2–3½ ft (60–105 cm). Leaves dark green. A fertile, well-drained soil in sun or part shade in a moist situation. The species is rarely grown, but there are many good varieties, often with double and scented flowers, 4–7 ins (10–18 cm) across. May–July.

Varieties

'Albert Crousse'. Pink. Double. Scented.
'August John'. Cherry-rose. Single.
'Baroness Schroeder'. White. Double. Scented.
'Bower of Roses'. Rose-crimson. Double.

Paeonia mascula	(*P. arietina*). Height 1½–2½ ft (45–75 cm). Leaves green, smooth above, hairy, grey-green beneath. Stems hairy with single pink flowers 3–5 ins (7.5–13 cm) across with yellow stamens. May–June.
Paeonia officinalis	'Rubra-plena'. Height 2–2½ ft (60–75 cm). Leaves deeply cut, green. Flowers crimson-red. Double. To 5 ins (13 cm) across. May–June.
Papaver orientalis	'Allegro'. (Oriental Poppy). Height 2–3 ft (60–90 cm). Plant spreading, forming clumps of coarse, hairy, deeply cut dark green leaves. Flowers 3½–4 ins (9–10 cm) across.
Phlox paniculata	'Prospero'. Height 2½–3½ ft (75–105 cm).
Polygonatum multiflorum	(*P. x hybridum*) (Solomon's Seal). Native. Height 2–3 ft (60–90 cm). Leaves smooth, green, oblong, clasping the stem. Flowers white 1 in (2.5 cm) long in clusters of 2–3. Berries, black. Easily grown in any soil. Sun or part shade.
Primula auricula	Varieties. Height 6 ins (15 cm). Leaves fleshy, pale green. Flowers in umbels, up to 1 in (2.5 cm) across. A well-drained humus-rich soil in a moist situation in sun or part shade. Many varieties and colours. 'Old Yellow Dusty Miller'. Yellow. 'Red Dusty Miller'. Red. 'Blue Fire'. Blue. 'Willowbrook'. Yellow.
Primula denticulata	(Drumstick Primrose). Height 1 ft (30 cm). Leaves pale green, broad, forming a compact rosette. Flowers on dense globular heads, 2–3 ins (5–7.5 cm) across. Colour variable, from blue, mauve, lilac, purple. 'Alba' is a good white form. Moisture loving plants. Sun or part shade. Ideal for boggy areas and pond-sides.
Primula vulgaris	(Primrose). Native. Height 6 ins (15 cm). Leaves light green, 3 ins (7.5 cm) long, wrinkled. Flowers yellow with deep yellow centres, 1 in (2.5 cm) across. March–May. Any fertile soil in a moist position. Sun or part shade.
Primula x polyanthus	Varieties. Garden hybrids derived *P. vulgaris* and *P. veris* and their coloured forms. Flowers to 1½ ins (4 cm) borne on trusses, on stout stems above the leaves. Any fertile soil in a moist situation in sun or part shade. A variety of colours available in different strains. 'Giant Bouquet' 'Monarch' Also for indoor pot cultivation: 'Mother's Day' 'Biedermeier'
Pulmonaria saccharata	'Highdown'. Height to 12 ins (30 cm). Leaves oval, spotted with silver-white. Flowers funnel-shaped, pink-blue, ¾ in (18 mm) long. March–April. Any soil in a moist situation in shade.

Rudbeckia newmanii	(*R. speciosa*) (*R. fulgida*). Height 2–3 ft (60–90 cm). Leaves, green, 6 ins (15 cm) long, toothed. Flowers yellow-orange, $2\frac{1}{2}$ ins (6.5 cm) across. July–Sept. Any well-drained soil in sun. Excellent for cut flowers.
Saxifraga umbrosa	(London Pride). Height 1 ft (30cm). Leaves dark green, thick, $2\frac{1}{2}$ ins (6.5 cm) long. Flowers star-shaped, pink in panicles 6 ins (15 cm) long. May. Any well-drained soil containing lime. A sunny position.
Sempervivum tectorum	(Common Houseleek). Height 2–3 ins (5–7.5 cm) spreading to 12 ins (30 cm). An evergreen succulent. Leaves fleshy in a rosette. Green with maroon tips. Flowers, pink-red, 1 in (2.5 cm) across. July. Any well-drained soil in sun.
Verbascum x hybridum	(Mullein). A hybrid between V. *pulverulentum* and V. *sinuatum*. *Variety* 'Gainsborough'. Height 3–4 ft (90–120 cm). Leaves grey, hairy. Flowers yellow, on spikes. June–August. Any well-drained soil in sun.
Viola odorata	(Sweet Violet). Native. Height 3–6 ins (7–15 cm). Plant, spreading, 1–$1\frac{1}{2}$ ft (30–45 cm). Leaves, heart-shaped, dark green. Flowers, blue-purple or white. Fragrant. February–April. A moist situation in sun or part shade. *Varieties* 'Christmas'. White. Early flowering. 'Czar'. Deep violet-purple. 'Sulphurea'. Apricot-yellow.
Viola tricolor	(Heartsease). Numerous varieties. Height 6–9 ins (15–23 cm). Plant spreading 1–$1\frac{1}{2}$ ft (30–45 cm). Leaves green, oval with rounded teeth. Flowers $\frac{1}{2}$–$1\frac{1}{2}$ ins (13–40 mm) wide. May–Sept. Any-well drained soil in a moist situation. Sun or part shade. *Varieties* 'Arkwright'. Crimson. Fragrant. 'Blue Heaven'. Blue with yellow eye. 'Clear Crystals'. Various colours. 'Goldie'. Golden Yellow.

Bulbs and Corms

Anemone blanda	Height to 6 ins (15 cm). Flowers blue, $1\frac{1}{2}$ ins (4 cm) across. Also mauve, pink and white forms. February–April. Any fertile soil in sun or part shade.
Anemone nemorosa	(Wood Anemone). Native. Height 6–8 ins (15–20 cm). Flowers white, often flushed mauve or pink on the outside, 1–$1\frac{1}{2}$ ins (2.5–4 cm) across. March–April. Any fertile soil in sun or part shade.

Crocus chrysanthus	Height 3–4 ins (7.5–10 cm). Flowers golden-yellow. February–March. The species is the parent of numerous species and, with other species, many hybrids. Any well-drained soil in sun or shade.
Crocus nudiflorus	(*C. cancellatus*). Leaves develop after flowers. Flowers, rounded 3½–5 ins (9–13 cm), purple. Sept–October. Any well-drained soil in sun or shade.
Cyclamen coum	(*C. ibericum*). Height 3 ins (7.5 cm). Leaves heart-shaped, dark green, often marbled with silver above. Flowers pink, crimson or white, ¾ in (18 mm) long. December–March.
Cyclamen europaeum	(*C. purpurascens*). Height 4 ins (10 cm). Leaves heart-shaped, green with silvery veining. Flowers carmine or pink, fragrant, ¾ in (18 mm) long. July–Sept.
Cyclamen neopolitanum	(*C. hederifolium*). Height 4 ins (10 cm). Leaves dark green with silvery markings, until May. Flowers 1 in (2.5 cm) long, vary from mauve to pale pink. Also white form, 'Album'. July–November. Cyclamen spp. Any well-drained, humus-rich soil in part shade.
Eranthis hyemalis	(Winter Aconite). Height 4 ins (10 cm). Leaves deeply cut, pale green. Flowers yellow, ¾–1 in (2–2.5 cm) across. January–March. A well-drained soil in a moist situation, sun or shade.
Erythronium dens-canis	(Dog's-tooth Violet). Height 6 ins (15 cm). Leaves blotched grey or brown. Flowers pink-purple. April–May. A variable species. A humus-rich soil in a moist situation, sun or part shade. *Many varieties* 'Lilac Wonder' 'Purple King' 'Pink Perfection' 'White Splendour'
Fritillaria imperialis	(Crown Imperial). Height 2–3 ft (60–90 cm). Leaves, glossy green in whorls up the stem. Flowers yellow to red, 2 ins (5 cm) long. April–May. Any fertile, well-drained soil in sun or part shade.
Fritillaria maleagris	(Snake's-head Fritillary). Native. Height 1–1½ ft (30–45 cm). Leaves thin, grass-like. Flowers bell-shaped, white with purple chequered markings, 1½ ins (4 cm) long. April–May. A moist situation, sun or part shade. *Variety* 'Alba'. White.
Galanthus nivalis	(Snowdrop). Native. Height 3–8 ins (7.5–20 cm). Leaves narrow, strap-shaped. Flowers white with green blotches on inner petals. January–March. Any fertile soil in part shade.
Lilium candidum	(Madonna Lily). Height 4–5 ft (120–150 cm). Leaves light green. Flowers trumpet-shaped, white, fragrant, 3–3½ ins (7.5–9 cm) long. June–July. Any soil in sun. Lime tolerant.
Lilium martagon	(Turk's-cap Lily). Height 4–5 ft (120–150 cm). Flowers rose-purple, 1–1½ ins (2.5–4 cm) long. July–August. Any soil in sun. Lime tolerant.

Narcissus cyclamineus	Height 6–8 ins (15–20 cm). Leaves dark green, thin. Flowers golden-yellow 2 ins (5 cm) long. February–March. A well-drained humus-rich soil in sun or part shade.
Narcissus pseudonarcissus	(Wild Daffodil). Native. Height 6–12 ins (15–30 cm). Leaves, strap-shaped. Flowers lemon-yellow trumpets, 2½ ins (6.5 cm) long. Petals, pale-yellow. March–April. Any well-drained, humus-rich soil in sun or part shade. *Variety* *N. pseudonarcissus moschatus*. White.
Ornithogalum umbellatum	(Star of Bethlehem). Native. Height 6 ins (15 cm). Leaves narrow, pointed, green. Flowers white with green outer stripes. April–May. Any well-drained soil in sun or part shade.
Tulipa silvestris	(Wild Tulip). Possibly native. 1–1½ ft (30–45 cm). Leaves narrow, green. Flowers golden-yellow or yellow-green, 2½ ins (6.5 cm) long, fragrant. April. A well-drained soil in sun or part shade.

Annuals and Biennials

Althaea rosea	(Hollyhock). Height 4½ ft (135 cm) annual, 9 ft (3 m) biennial. Leaves, light green, rough and hairy with lobes. Flowers single and double in shades of pink, 4–5 ins (10–13 cm) across on rigid stems. July–Sept. A heavy fertile soil in a sunny, sheltered position. Water freely during dry weather.
Alyssum maritimum	'Carpet of Snow'. Height 4–6 ins (10–15 cm). Plant densely branched with narrow grey-green leaves. Flowers white. June–Sept. Any well-drained soil in full sun.
Antirrhinum majus	(Snapdragon). Many different varieties which have replaced the type. Divided into 3 groups according to height. *Antirrhinum m. maximum*. Height 3–4 ft (90–120 cm). 'Apple Blossom'. Pink. 'Cavalier'. Orange and pink. 'Sunlight'. Yellow. 'White Spire'. White. *Antirrhinum m. nanum*. Height 1½ ft (45 cm). 'Black Prince'. Crimson. 'Monarch Orange' 'Yellow Monarch' 'Pink Lavender' *Antirrhinum m. pumilum*. Height 4–8 ins (10–20 cm). 'Tom Thumb Mixed' 'Floral Carpet Mixed' Any well-drained, fertile soil in sun or part shade.

Calendula officinalis — (Pot Marigold). Height 1–2 ft (30–60 cm). Plant, bushy, erect. Leaves light green, long, narrow and aromatic. Flowers 4 ins (10 cm) across, daisy-like. Any soil in a sunny position. Many varieties and colours. 'Pacific Beauty'. Mixed or separate colours.

Centaurea cyanus — (Cornflower). Native. Height 6 in–2½ ft (15–75 cm). Plant erect. Leaves grey-green. Flowers blue. 1–2 ins (2.5–5 cm) across.
Variety
'Blue Diadem'. 2–3 ft (60–90 cm). Large flowers.

Cheiranthus cheiri — (Wallflower). Height 6 in–2 ft (15–60 cm). Plant, erect. Leaves dark green, narrow. Flowers ½–1 in (13–25 mm) across in dense spikes. April–June. Any well-drained soil in a sunny position.
Numerous varieties and colours
'Blood Red'. Height 1½ ft (45 cm).
'Cloth of Gold'. Height 1½ ft (45 cm). Golden yellow.
'Fair Lady Mixed'. Height 1½ ft (45 cm).
'Persian Carpet'. Mixed shades.
'Orange Bedder'. Height 9–12 ins (23–30 cm).
'Scarlet Bedder'. Height 9–12 ins (23–30 cm).
'Tom Thumb Mixed'. Height 9–12 ins (23–30 cm).

Delphinium consolida — (Larkspur). Height 3–4 ft (90–120 cm). Leaves green, segmented. Flowers in racemes 9–15 ins (23–40 cm) long. A deep, fertile soil in sun, in a sheltered position. Many varieties and strains. The Giant Imperial strain is available in a wide range of colours.

Dianthus barbatus — (Sweet William). Height 6 in–1½ ft (15–45 cm). Flowers densely packed 3–5 ins (7.5–13 cm) across.
Many varieties, including:
'Dwarf Double Mixed'. Height 1 ft (30 cm).
'Indian Carpet'. Height 1 ft (30 cm).
'Messenger Mixed'. Height 1½ ft (45 cm).
Any well-drained soil with lime. A sunny position.

Digitalis purpurea — (Foxglove). Native. Height 3–5 ft (1–1.5 m). Leaves oblong, dark green in a rosette. Flowers in spikes, pink-purple or white. Spotted. June–July. Any soil in sun or part shade.

Helianthus annus — (Sunflower). Height 3–10 ft (1–3 m). Leaves heart-shaped. Flowers 12 ins (30 cm) or more across. Yellow petals with large brown or purple discs. July–Sept. Any well-drained soil in a sunny position. Support tall plants.

Iberis umbellata — (Candytuft). Height 6–12 ins (15–30 cm). Leaves narrow, green. Flowers white and pale purple. June–Sept. Any soil in sun.
Variety
'Dwarf Fairy Mixed'. Height 10 ins (25 cm).

Lathyrus odoratus — (Sweet Pea). Height 5–10 ft (1.5–3 m). Leaves in pairs, green, oval. Leaf stalk ending with a tendril. Flowers, fragrant, 1–2 ins (2.5–5 cm) across. Pink, white or purple. June–Sept.

Lunaria annua	(Honesty). Height 2–3 ft (60–90 cm). Leaves heart-shaped. Coarsely toothed. Flowers purple, fragrant, ½ in (13 mm) across. April–June. Followed by flattened silvery-green seed pods. Any well-drained soil in part shade.
Malcolmia maritima	(Virginian Stock). Height 8 ins (20 cm). Leaves grey-green. Flowers red, lilac, pink or white, ½ in (13 mm) across, fragrant, 6–8 weeks after sowing. Any soil in sun or part shade.
Myosotis sylvatica	(Forget-me-not). Native. Stem and leaves hairy. Flowers blue, fragrant, ⅓ in (10 mm) across. May–June. Any soil or situation, but best in moist humus-rich soil in part shade.
Nigella damascena	(Love-in-a-mist). Height 2 ft (60 cm). Plant erect, with finely cut foliage. Flowers blue or white, 1½ in (41 mm) across. June–August. Seed pod 1 in (2.5 cm) long. Brown with red bars. Any well-drained soil in sun.
Oenothera biennis	(Evening Primrose). Height 3 ft (1 m). Leaves narrow, pointed. Stems erect. Flowers pale yellow, 1½–2 ins (4–5 cm) across. June–October. Any well-drained soil in sun.
Pelargonium	(Pot geranium). Numerous varieties but most traditional are 'Paul Crampel' and 'Salmon Crampel'.
Phlox drummondii	Height 15 ins (40 cm). Stems erect with light green leaves. Flowers on dense heads, 3–4 ins (7.5–10 cm) across, in shades of pink, purple, blue, red and white. July–Sept. Any fertile, well-drained soil in a sunny position.
Scabiosa atropurpurea	(Sweet scabious). Height 3 ft (1 m). Leaves, narrow, deeply cut in a rosette. Flowers crimson, 2 ins (5 cm) across. June–Sept. Any fertile, well-drained soil in sun.
Tropaeolum majus	(Nasturtium). Height 8 ft (2.5 m). A climbing/trailing plant. Leaves green, circular with wavy edges. Flowers yellow or orange, fragrant, 2 ins (5 cm) across with long spur. Leaves and stems aromatic when crushed. June–Sept. Any soil in a sunny position.

Herbs

Borage	(*Borago officinalis*). Height 2–3 ft (60–90 cm). Plant covered in silver-grey hairs. Flowers blue, star-shaped. A medicinal herb.
Chamomile	(*Anthemis nobilis*). Height to 12 ins (30 cm). Flowers white with gold centre. A medicinal herb.

Chives	(*Allium schoenoprasum*). Native. Height, 6–10 ins (15–25 cm). Leaves slender, onion-like. Flowers rose-pink in dense round heads, 1–2 ins (2.5–5 cm) across. June–July. A culinary herb.
Comfrey	(*Symphytum officinale*). Height to 3 ft (90 cm). Leaves dark green. Flowers white, pink or purple. Any fertile soil in a moist shaded position. A medicinal herb.
Cotton Lavender	(*Santolina chamaecyparissus*). Height 18–24 ins (45–60 cm). Leaves silvery, woolly, finely cut. Flowers lemon-yellow. July. A medicinal herb.
Dill	(*Anethum graveolens*). Height 2–3 ft (60–90 cm). Leaves, feathery. Flowers yellow. June–July. Medicinal and culinary herb.
Feverfew	(*Chrysanthemum parthenium*). Height 1–1½ ft (30–45 cm). Bushy habit, leaves pale green, strongly aromatic. Flowers, many, white with yellow centres, ¾ in (18 mm) across. Any soil in sun or part shade. A medicinal herb.
Good King Henry	(*Chenopodium bonus-henricus*). Height to 2 ft (60 cm). Leaves arrow-shaped. Flowers yellow-green. Medicinal and culinary herb.
Hyssop	(*Hyssopus officinalis*). Height 1–2 ft (30–60 cm). Evergreen. Flowers red, blue or white. June–October. A medicinal herb.
Lady's Mantle	(*Alchemilla vulgaris*). Height to 12 ins (30 cm). Leaves 6 ins (15 cm) across, grey, hairy. Flowers in clusters, yellow-green. June–August. A medicinal herb.
Lemon Balm	(*Melissa officinalis*). Height 2–3 ft (60–90 cm). Leaves, fragrant lemon when crushed. Flowers white. June–October. Medicinal and culinary herb.
Marjoram	(*Origanum vulgare*). Height 1–2 ft (30–60 cm). Leaves aromatic. Flowers red-purple. June–August. Medicinal and culinary herb.
Meadowsweet	(*Filipendula ulmaria*). Height to 4 ft (120 cm). Leaves dark green. Flowers white, fragrant. June–Sept. A medicinal herb.
Mint	Spearmint (M. *spicata*) Peppermint (M. *piperita*) Pennyroyal (M. *pulegium*) Water Mint (M. *aquatica*) The above mints all have aromatic foliage and flowers in various shades of blue, lilac and purple. Spearmint (Garden Mint) is a widely used culinary herb and all four have medicinal properties. They grow best in a moist situation in sun or part shade.
Myrtle	(*Myrtus communis*). Height to 10 ft (3 m). Evergreen, aromatic. Flowers fragrant, white. Berries black. A culinary herb.
Parsley	(*Petroselinum crispum*). Many varieties. This well-known herb needs no description. It has many uses, both medicinal and culinary.

Rosemary	(*Rosmarinus officinalis*). Height to 5 ft (1.5 m). Leaves, narrow, evergreen, aromatic. Flowers blue. April–May. Medicinal and culinary herb.
Rue	(*Ruta graveolens*). Height to 3 ft (90 cm). Evergreen. Leaves blue-green. Flowers yellow-green. June–Sept. Medicinal and culinary herb.
Sage	(*Salvia officinalis*). Height 1–2 ft (30–60 cm). Leaves grey-green, hairy. Flowers blue, purple or white. August. Medicinal and culinary herb.
Savoury (summer)	(*Satureja hortensis*). Height 1–1½ ft (30–45 cm). A hairy annual, aromatic. Flowers pink, purple or white. July. A culinary herb.
Savoury (winter)	(*Satureja montana*). Height 1–1½ ft (30–45 cm). Perennial. Flowers purple on spikes. June–July. A culinary herb.
Southernwood	(*Artemisia abrotanum*). Height to 3 ft (90 cm). Leaves grey-green, finely divided. Flowers yellow-white. A medicinal herb.
Sweet Basil	(*Ocimum basilicum*). Height 1–2 ft (30–60 cm). Leaves grey-green below, dotted above, often purplish. Aromatic. Flowers white. Medicinal and culinary herb.
Sweet Rocket	(*Hesperis matronalis*). Height 2–3 ft (60–90 cm). Flowers fragrant, purple, lilac or white, ½–1 in (13–25 mm) across. May–June. Old medicinal and culinary herb.
Thyme	The following species and varieties, including the hybrid *x citriodorous*, are all hardy, evergreen and aromatic, growing best in an open sunny situation. Medicinal and culinary herbs.
T. x citriodorous	Height 9–12 ins (23–30 cm). Lemon-scented. Flowers pale pink. June–August.
T. serpyllum	(Wild Thyme). Height 1–3 ins (2.5–7.5 cm). Flowers, shades of red to white. June–August. *Varieties* 'Albus'. White. 'Annie Hall'. Pale pink. 'Coccineus'. Crimson.
T. vulgaris	Height 4–8ins (10–20 cm). Flowers mauve. June. *Variety* 'Aureus'. Golden-yellow foliage.
Woodruff	(*Galium odoratum*). Height 4–10 ins (10–25 cm). Leaves bright green in whorls. Flowers white, fragrant. May–June. A medicinal herb. A humus-rich soil in part shade.

Suppliers of Plants and Materials for Cottage Gardens

(All supply by mail order unless otherwise indicated)

Perennial plants, bulbs, shrubs, climbers, fruit

Spalding Bulb Co.,
Spalding, Lincolnshire

Hortico,
Spalding, Lincolnshire

Perennial plants

Bressingham Gardens,
Bressingham, Diss,
Norfolk IP22 2AB

Paeonies and Iris

Kelways Nurseries,
Langport, Somerset TA10 9SL

Pinks

Ramparts Nurseries,
Bakers Lane, Braiswick,
Colchester, Essex CO4 5BD

Three Counties Nurseries,
Marshwood, Bridport,
Dorset DT6 5QJ

Seeds

Hurst Seeds,
Witham, Essex CM8 2DX

Mr. Fothergill's Seeds,
Regal Lodge, Gazeley Rd.,
Kentford, Newmarket,
Suffolk CB8 7QB

Bulbs

Van Tubergen,
Oldfield Lane,
Wisbech, Cambs PE13 2RJ

Roses

John Mattock Ltd,
Nuneham Courtenay,
Oxford OX9 9PY

Peter Beales Roses
London Rd, Attleborough,
Norfolk

David Austin Roses,
Bowling Green Lane,
Albrighton,
Wolverhampton WV7 3HB

Trees, shrubs and climbers

Notcutts Nurseries Ltd,
Woodbridge, Suffolk

A. E. Roberts Ltd.,
Wickham, Hampshire

Nettletons Nursery,
Ivy Mill Lane,
Godstone, Surrey
(No mail order)

Herbs

Iden Croft Nurseries
& Herb Farm,
Frittenden Rd, Staplehurst,
Kent

Soft fruit

Ken Muir,
Honeypot Farm,
Weeley Heath,
Clacton-on-Sea,
Essex CO16 9BJ

Paving and walling

Bradstone Garden Products,
Okus, Swindon, Wilts SN1 4JJ
(Supply through stockists)

Aquatic plants and pond equipment

Stapeley Water Gardens Ltd,
Stapeley, Nantwich,
Cheshire CW5 7JA

Submersible pumps

Hozelock Ltd,
Haddenham, Aylesbury, Bucks

Clay flower pots

C. H. Brannam Ltd,
Litchdon Potteries,
Barnstaple, Devon
(Supply through stockists)

Pebbles and shingle

Border Stone,
Middletown, Welshpool, Powys
(Supply through stockists)

Original ornaments and sculpture

Malcolm Pollard
42 East Park Parade,
Northampton NN1 4LA

Beehives and equipment

E. H. Taylor Ltd,
Beehive Works, Welwyn,
Herts AL6 0AZ

Picture Credits

THE AUTHOR and publishers would like to thank the following for the use of their photographs on the pages listed.

Geest Horticultural Group; pages 50, 51 (left), 70 (bottom), 71 (bottom right and left), 86 (bottom), 94 (top right and bottom right), 95 (top left and bottom), 98, 102, 106. Greetings cards reproducing the paintings on pages 11, 15, 18 and 47 have been published by The Bucentaur Gallery Limited and the paintings are reproduced here by courtesy of David Jackson Esq.: 11; The Priory Gallery: 15; Christopher Wood Ltd, London: 18; 47 formerly in the Collection of The Leger Galleries Ltd, London, Patrick Johns: 39, 55 (right), 67, 70 (top), 71 (top left), 78 (bottom right and left), 79 (top), 94 (bottom left), 95 (top right), 118 (top). The Harry Smith Horticultural Photographic Collection: frontispiece, 42, 43, 51 (left), 54 (right), 55 (left), 63 (top right and bottom left), 66 (bottom left and right), 71 (top right), 78 (top left), 87 (top left and bottom), 94 (top left), 111 (bottom), 114, 115, 119, 122, 123, 126, 127, 130, 131, 135. The Merrist Wood College at the Chelsea Show: 27 (top), 30 and 31 (photographs taken by Derek Goard). Graham Richardson: 7, 22, 34, 35, 38, 39 (top), 78 (top right), 79 (bottom), 86 (top left and right). Bradstone Garden Products: 26, 27 (bottom). John Mattock Ltd: 62 (top and bottom left), 63 (bottom right). David Austen: 66 (bottom right and left). Peter Beales Roses: 62 (top and bottom right), 63 (top left). Bulb Information Desk: 103, 107, 110. Michael Warren: 46. The RHS Lindley Library for permission to photograph illustrations from *Wild Flowers of the British Isles* by H. Isabel Adams, 31, 82, 83, 91, 101 and, in black and white, from *Parkinson's Paradisi in Sole* and *The Florilegum* by Emanuel Sweerts (photographs taken by Godfrey New). Jarrolds: 14. The National Trust: 19.

Index